Reflective Empowerment

EMPOWER YOURSELF

PHILIP GUY ROCHFORD

BALBOA.
PRESS

A DIVISION OF HAY HOUSE

Balboa Press books may be ordered through booksellers or by contacting:

Balboa Press
A Division of Hay House
1663 Liberty Drive
Bloomington, IN 47403
www.balboapress.com
1 (877) 407-4847

Print information available on the last page.

ISBN: 978-1-5043-8189-5 (sc)
ISBN: 978-1-5043-8190-1 (e)

Balboa Press rev. date: 06/16/2017

DEDICATION

Thousands of persons have crossed my path in life. Some
have enriched my life, and in turn, I have enriched many
lives. *Reflective Empowerment* is one of the outcomes
of these interactions, and so this book is dedicated to
all who have helped me on my life's journey.

CONTENTS

Dedication v

Commentary on the best way to use this book xxix

Introduction... xxxi

CHAPTER 1: LOOK WITHIN 1

WEEK 1 2

    REFLECTION 1. You can transcend your despondency 2

    REFLECTION 2. Believe beyond the present moment 3

    REFLECTION 3. Beyond hope 4

    REFLECTION 4. Building relationships 5

    REFLECTION 5. Pain is a barometer for action.....................6

    Day 6 review 8

    Day 7 review 9

WEEK 2 10

    REFLECTION 6. Cherish and polish your gift of speech 10

    REFLECTION 7. Five Pillars of Commitment for your
                   success...10

    REFLECTION 8. Mistakes are necessary for success..........12

REFLECTION 9. Transcend wrong opinions others
    have of you 12
REFLECTION 10. Think and plan instead of worrying....... 13
Day 6 review 15
Day 7 review 16

WEEK 3 17
REFLECTION 11. The best and worst of life 17
REFLECTION 12. Build your self-confidence.................... 18
REFLECTION 13. The gap in your life must be purposeful ... 19
REFLECTION 14. Upgrade your belief system.................... 20
REFLECTION 15. Use mistakes as stepping-stones to
    success... 21
Day 6 review 23
Day 7 review 24

WEEK 4 25
REFLECTION 16. Learn from losing.................................. 25
REFLECTION 17. Did you take action for success last
    week? 26
REFLECTION 18. Act now for your progress or success..... 27
REFLECTION 19. What is your story? 28
REFLECTION 20. Risk failure to get a chance of
    succeeding.. 29
Day 6 review 30
Day 7 review 31

WEEK 5 32

    REFLECTION 21. Relieve your stress................................32

    REFLECTION 22. Continue the year with strong success...33

    REFLECTION 23. The power of forgiveness 34

    REFLECTION 24. Honor your commitments 36

    REFLECTION 25. Power of your mind...............................37

    Day 6 review 38

    Day 7 review 39

WEEK 6 40

    REFLECTION 26. How serious are you about your success...40

    REFLECTION 27. Be empowered and awakened 41

    REFLECTION 28. Keep your journal of gratitude...............42

    REFLECTION 29. Shift to a different and better life...........43

    REFLECTION 30. Choices you make today shape your

                   future...45

    Day 6 review 46

    Day 7 review 47

WEEK 7 49

    REFLECTION 31. Nurture your unique talents 49

    REFLECTION 32. Re-visit your goals 50

    REFLECTION 33.Reach for greater success. 51

    REFLECTION 34. Release your brilliance..........................51

    REFLECTION 35. Your actions mirror your thoughts 53

    Day 6 review 54

    Day 7 review 55

WEEK 8 56

   REFLECTION 36. Rise to the world economic challenge....56

   REFLECTION 37. Towards self-mastery................................57

   REFLECTION 38. What are your concerns about your life?..58

   REFLECTION 39. Clarify what you stand for.....................59

   REFLECTION 40. Every difficulty has within it new opportunities 60

   Day 6 review 61

   Day 7 review 62

WEEK 9 63

   REFLECTION 41. Give that which you want, and you will receive it...63

   REFLECTION 42. Re-invent yourself.................................. 64

   REFLECTION 43. Think and act for success......................65

   REFLECTION 44. Your actions today determine your life tomorrow.......................................66

   REFLECTION 45. There is opportunity and possibility in every calamity................................67

   Day 6 review 68

   Day 7 review 69

CHAPTER 2: RISE TO THE CHALLENGE.................71

WEEK 10 72

   REFLECTION 46. Are you blessed? 72

   REFLECTION 47. Be Respectful to be successful...............73

REFLECTION 48. All things are possible..........................74

REFLECTION 49. Challenging success techniques............75

REFLECTION 50. Relentless focus helps you achieve
your goals..76

Day 6 review 77

Day 7 review 78

WEEK 11 79

REFLECTION 51. Your Champion's Creed.........................79

REFLECTION 52. Change your thoughts to change
your life 80

REFLECTION 53. Core values facilitate your success.........81

REFLECTION 54. Reflecting on your motives....................81

REFLECTION 55. Prepare to accomplish your desires........83

Day 6 review 84

Day 7 review 85

WEEK 12 86

REFLECTION 56. Step into your greatness.........................86

REFLECTION 57. Celebrate your achievements..................86

REFLECTION 58. People problems 88

REFLECTION 59. Personal vision and action revolution.....88

REFLECTION 60. Your uniqueness and individuality.........89

Day 6 review 91

Day 7 review 92

WEEK 13 94

REFLECTION 61.The Power of Fear..................................94

REFLECTION 62. Re-program your thinking 95

REFLECTION 63. What is your dream? 96

REFLECTION 64. Seize the moment...............................97

REFLECTION 65. A blend of habit and reasoning
balance your life 98

Day 6 review 99

Day 7 review 100

WEEK 14 101

REFLECTION 66. Take action when opportunity knocks.... 101

REFLECTION 67. What will you achieve in the next
five years? 102

REFLECTION 68. Thanksgiving 103

REFLECTION 69. Time is a precious gift that allows
your fulfillment..................................105

REFLECTION 70. Become part of the learning revolution... 105

Day 6 review 107

Day 7 review 108

WEEK 15 109

REFLECTION 71. Use your talents wisely.......................109

REFLECTION 72. Wealth and poverty can be both
blessings 110

REFLECTION 73. What "word" leads to growth in
your success?..................................... 110

REFLECTION 74. Commit your energy to what you
truly believe..................................... 111

REFLECTION 75. Your golden victory is to conquer yourself... 112

Day 6 review 113

Day 7 review 114

WEEK 16 115

REFLECTION 76. Reaching beyond your frustration........ 115

REFLECTION 77. Your invisible and invisible life............ 116

REFLECTION 78. From Achiever to Champion Achiever ... 117

REFLECTION 79. Act today for success........................... 118

REFLECTION 80. Are you spending your time wisely?.... 119

Day 6 review 121

Day 7 review 122

WEEK 17 123

REFLECTION 81. Be conscious of your dreams...............123

REFLECTION 82. Be purposeful..123

REFLECTION 83. Be tolerant of others' faults 124

REFLECTION 84. Choose to be better 125

REFLECTION 85. Act from love and win the commitment of others 126

Day 6 review 127

Day 7 review 128

WEEK 18 129

REFLECTION 86. Beyond the obvious.............................129

REFLECTION 87. Build your self esteem.........................129

REFLECTION 88. Design a better life for yourself 130

REFLECTION 89. Your decisions of destiny 131

REFLECTION 90. Brighten another's path, and you
brighten your own 132

Day 6 review 133

Day 7 review 134

WEEK 19 136

REFLECTION 91. Don't let others steal your dreams 136

REFLECTION 92. Your thoughts define you 136

REFLECTION 93. Shine brightly 138

REFLECTION 94. Speak to enhance your success 139

REFLECTION 95. Come together, work together and
grow together and we will succeed
together... 140

Day 6 review 141

Day 7 review 142

CHAPTER 3: KNOW YOUR DESTINATION 143

WEEK 20 144

REFLECTION 96. Break down your goals into several
convenient steps 144

REFLECTION 97. Dare to face your fear.......................... 144

REFLECTION 98. Find your "why' of living.................... 145

REFLECTION 99. Give freely of yourself 146

REFLECTION 100. Your thoughts s empower you or
imprison you 147

Day 6 review 148

Day 7 review 149

WEEK 21 150

REFLECTION 101. You can achieve your goals 150

REFLECTION 102. Your feelings influence your destiny 151

REFLECTION 103. From knowledge to action and wealth... 151

REFLECTION 104. Learn, embrace and focus 152

REFLECTION 105. Attention to details generates success ... 153

Day 6 review 155

Day 7 review 156

WEEK 22 157

REFLECTION 106. Live life fully 157

REFLECTION 107. Serve others to generate your own
purpose 158

REFLECTION 108. When opportunity knocks 158

REFLECTION 109. Patience Powers Progress 159

REFLECTION 110. Model nature's patience in pursuing
your goals 161

Day 6 review 162

Day 7 review 163

WEEK 23 164

REFLECTION 111. The insurmountable situation 164

REFLECTION 112. Power to live graciously 164

REFLECTION 113. Press on despite difficulties 165

REFLECTION 114. The price of success 166

REFLECTION 115. Proper preparation generates success 167

Day 6 review 168

Day 7 review 169

WEEK 24 170

REFLECTION 116. Prosperity is your birthright 170

REFLECTION 117. Take a stand for yourself 171

REFLECTION 118. Pursue your vision relentlessly 172

REFLECTION 119. Adopt a self-image of success 172

REFLECTION 120. Passion, focus, and intensity,
manifest your desires 173

Day 6 review 175

Day 7 review 176

WEEK 25 178

REFLECTION 121.Take a new step 178

REFLECTION 122. Unfold your greatness 179

REFLECTION 123. Use your power of choice 180

REFLECTION 124. Use your talents fully 181

REFLECTION 125. Persistence and commitment
ensure success 182

Day 6 review 183

Day 7 review 184

WEEK 26 185

REFLECTION 126. Want more in your life? 185

REFLECTION 127. Are you stopping your progress in
life? 186

REFLECTION 128. Why am I alive today? 186

REFLECTION 129. You are alive 187

REFLECTION 130. Your destination is strewn with
rough roads 188

Day 6 review 189

Day 7 review 190

WEEK 27 191

REFLECTION 131. Quiet your mind 191

REFLECTION 132. Your actions mould your life 192

REFLECTION 133. Strengthen your vision 192

REFLECTION 134. Slay procrastination 194

REFLECTION 135. The benefits and price of success 194

Day 6 review 196

Day 7 review 197

WEEK 28 198

REFLECTION 136. Your struggles facilitate your success ... 198

REFLECTION 137. Read daily to excel 199

REFLECTION 138. Everything vibrates, but at different
rates 199

REFLECTION 139. Habits form your future 201

REFLECTION 140. Working selflessly for others
makes love visible 202

Day 6 review 203

Day 7 review 204

WEEK 29 205

REFLECTION 141. Achieve through small regular steps 205

REFLECTION 142. Success requires activity 206

REFLECTION 143. Your desired results 206

REFLECTION 144. Act in love 207

REFLECTION 145. Your life is created decision by
decision 208

Day 6 review 209

Day 7 review 210

CHAPTER 4: YOU ARE THE STAR OF YOUR SHOW

CHAPTER 4: YOU ARE THE STAR OF YOUR
SHOW 211

WEEK 30 212

REFLECTION 146. Experiment with achievement...........212

REFLECTION 147. Work your dream 213

REFLECTION 148. Focus and wisely manage your
daily activities 214

REFLECTION 149. Action versus thinking 215

REFLECTION 150. Your web of ideas determines your
success or failure............................... 216

Day 6 review 218

Day 7 review 219

WEEK 31 221

REFLECTION 151. Pursue your ideas to be your best.......221

REFLECTION 152. Break down your major goal into
sub-goals 221

REFLECTION 153. Strive for better relationships 222

REFLECTION 154. Activate your personal efforts...........223

REFLECTION 155. Your value increases, when you do
more than is expected......................224
Day 6 review 226
Day 7 review 227

WEEK 32 228
REFLECTION 156. Your values govern your choices........228
REFLECTION 157. How are you responding to life 229
REFLECTION 158. A breakthrough in your life...............229
REFLECTION 159. Set your sails for success 230
REFLECTION 160. Take care of trifles and you settle
your life's design 230
Day 6 review 232
Day 7 review 233

WEEK 33 234
REFLECTION 161. Is a Lifestyle Coach necessary?..........234
REFLECTION 162. You are the pivot for your success......235
REFLECTION 163. Your experiences fashion your life 236
REFLECTION 164. Your life 5 years from now.................237
REFLECTION 165. Pursue new possibilities to find a
better way 238
Day 6 review 240
Day 7 review 241

WEEK 34 242
REFLECTION 166. Act on your knowledge 242
REFLECTION 167. Is your past haunting you? 243

REFLECTION 168. Fulfill your desires 244

REFLECTION 169. Have a better vision for your life 244

REFLECTION 170. What you expect with confidence
tends to materialize 245

Day 6 review 247

Day 7 review 248

WEEK 35 249

REFLECTION 171. Old habits are not easily changed 249

REFLECTION 172. Your response to life.........................250

REFLECTION 173. Have singleness of purpose 251

REFLECTION 174. Roadblocks to success 252

REFLECTION 175. To be victorious you must believe
in your cause 253

Day 6 review 254

Day 7 review 255

WEEK 36 256

REFLECTION 176. The challenges of relationships...........256

REFLECTION 177. Sweep your mind clean.....................257

REFLECTION 178. Negative self-talk does not help you...258

REFLECTION 179. Glimpse your brilliance 258

REFLECTION 180. Learn from your errors, and move on ...260

Day 6 review 261

Day 7 review 262

WEEK 37 264

REFLECTION 181. Accept yourself, and strive to make
better decisions......................................264

REFLECTION 182. Do something different, if you
want different results........................264

REFLECTION 183. Get sufficient information a before
you move to the level of decision 265

REFLECTION 184. Great discoveries occur through
visioning..266

REFLECTION 185. Learn to face and confront your fear.....267

Day 6 review 268

Day 7 review 269

CHAPTER 5: CHOOSE WISELY 271

WEEK 38 272

REFLECTION 186. Accept the consequences of your
choices..272

REFLECTION 187. Appreciate what you have,.................272

REFLECTION 188. Smell the roses on life's journey.........273

REFLECTION 189. Happiness is different from pleasure.....274

REFLECTION 190. Give, sow and contribute for your
prosperity 275

Day 6 review 276

Day 7 review 277

WEEK 39 278

    REFLECTION 191. Desires and core values are interrelated 278

    REFLECTION 192. Imagination is integral to accomplishment..................................278

    REFLECTION 193. Plan and plant your dreams 279

    REFLECTION 194. How to get to your next higher level 280

    REFLECTION 195. Accomplish your goals daily and experience it's joy 280

    Day 6 review 282

    Day 7 review 283

WEEK 40 284

    REFLECTION 196. Emphasize right things in life to get right results....................................284

    REFLECTION 197. Use picture words for powerful communication..................................284

    REFLECTION 198. What is the life you really want?........285

    REFLECTION 199. Inspire others to blossom...................286

    REFLECTION 200. If your mind tells you can, then you can 287

    Day 6 review 288

    Day 7 review 289

WEEK 41 290

    REFLECTION 201. Increase your knowledge for greater success 290

REFLECTION 202. Engage in worthwhile activity for your success 290

REFLECTION 203. Actions produce your banquet of consequences...291

REFLECTION 204. Your innermost beliefs will take you over troubled waters 292

REFLECTION 205. Compromise and tolerance support your success 293

Day 6 review 294

Day 7 review 295

CHAPTER 6: BE EMPOWERED AND RELEASE YOUR BRILLIANCE

CHAPTER 6: BE EMPOWERED AND RELEASE YOUR BRILLIANCE..297

WEEK 42 298

REFLECTION 206. Successful people do not quit because of their mistakes 298

REFLECTION 207. Are you modeling or living aimlessly?..298

REFLECTION 208. Character Traits of Successful People...299

REFLECTION 209. Dialogue your ideas to be successful 300

REFLECTION 210. Monologue and dialogue - Part I 302

Day 6 review 303

Day 7 review 304

WEEK 43 306

REFLECTION 211. Monologue and dialogue - Part II 306

REFLECTION 212. Ask good questions – Part I 307

REFLECTION 213. Ask good questions – Part II 307
REFLECTION 214. Meaning of success – Part I................308
REFLECTION 215. Meaning of success – Part II 309
Day 6 review 310
Day 7 review 311

WEEK 44 312
REFLECTION 216. Stagnancy or transformation?.............312
REFLECTION 217. Become more of a spiritual adept 313
REFLECTION 218. Transform yourself for success –
                Part I.. 314
REFLECTION 219. Transform yourself for success –
                Part II 315
REFLECTION 220. Re-engineering for more success –
                Part I.. 316
Day 6 review 318
Day 7 review 319

WEEK 45 320
REFLECTION 221. Re-engineering for more success –
                Part II 320
REFLECTION 222. Re-engineering for more success –
                Part III 321
REFLECTION 223. Re-engineering for more success –
                Part IV 321
REFLECTION 224. Better personal connections
                generate success - Part I....................322

REFLECTION 225. Better personal connections
                generate success - Part II 323
Day 6 review 324
Day 7 review 325

WEEK 46 326
REFLECTION 226. Better personal connections
                generate success - Part III 326
REFLECTION 227. Forms of intelligence 327
REFLECTION 228. Angles of personal development –
                Part I 327
REFLECTION 229. Angles of personal development –
                Part II 329
REFLECTION 230. Your consciousness influences
                your success – Part I 330
Day 6 review 331
Day 7 review 332

WEEK 47 333
REFLECTION 231. Your consciousness influences your
                success – Part II 333
REFLECTION 232. Your consciousness influences
                your success – Part III 334
REFLECTION 233. Your consciousness influences
                your success – Part IV 334
REFLECTION 234. Your consciousness influences
                your success – Part V 335

REFLECTION 235. The magic that is success – Part I 336
Day 6 review 337
Day 7 review 338

WEEK 48 339
REFLECTION 236. The magic that is success – Part II.....339
REFLECTION 237. The magic that is success – Part III....340
REFLECTION 238. The magic that is success – Part IV ...340
REFLECTION 239. The magic that is success – Part V.....341
REFLECTION 240. Beyond success 342
Day 6 review 344
Day 7 review 345

WEEK 49 347
REFLECTION 241. Success through a sense of self –
        Part I..347
REFLECTION 242. Success through a sense of self –
        Part II 347
REFLECTION 243. Success through a sense of self –
        Part III...348
REFLECTION 244. Success through a sense of self –
        Part IV...349
REFLECTION 245. Success through a sense of self –
        Part V..350
Day 6 review 351
Day 7 review 352

WEEK 50 353

    REFLECTION 246. Success through a sense of self –
                Part VI 353

    REFLECTION 247. Your reality map limits your
                success – Part I 353

    REFLECTION 248. Your reality map limits your
                success – Part II 354

    REFLECTION 249. Your reality map limits your
                success – Part III 355

    REFLECTION 250. Your reality map limits your
                success – Part IV 356

    Day 6 review 357

    Day 7 review 358

WEEK 51 360

    REFLECTION 251. Your reality map limits your
                success – Part V 360

    REFLECTION 252. Questions drive your success – Part I ... 360

    REFLECTION 253. Questions drive your success –
                Part II 361

    REFLECTION 254. Questions drive your success –
                Part III 362

    REFLECTION 255. Questions drive your success –
                Part IV 363

    Day 6 review 365

    Day 7 review 366

WEEK 52 367
    REFLECTION 256. Questions drive your success –
        Part V 367
    REFLECTION 257. Illusion and success – Part I 368
    REFLECTION 258. Illusion and success – Part II 369
    REFLECTION 259. The inner game of success – Part I 369
    REFLECTION 260. The inner game of success – Part II...370
    Day 6 review 372
    Day 7 review 373

Overall Conclusion...375

COMMENTARY ON THE BEST WAY TO USE THIS BOOK

You want to design the best life for yourself. If you are building a house, you take one step, then another, and you continue the momentum until the house is completed. Building your life is similar. You need to consider and make changes step by step. You have to change old habits that no longer serve your best interests. You have to introduce new habits that will empower you.

Reflective Empowerment facilitates building an internal structure that gives you a mind set to release your potential and greatness. A key is to reflect on the content as you read along, and act on the elements that empower you to success. It is not merely reading for information. You have to be proactive in responding to what you read in a structured, consistent manner.

Reflective Empowerment is designed as a one-year program to increase your personal empowerment. There are 52 weeks in a year, and there is a different Empowerment Reflection for the first five days of each week, with review and action steps for you to take on the 6th and 7th day of each week.

To achieve the best results, read the book continuously the first time to get a sense of the overall program. On completion of your first reading, start over, and read only one Reflection each day, and really absorb and reflect on what you read. On the 6th day of the week review what you read for the previous 5 days and document what you are taking away from that week's reflections to improve your life. Space is provided in the appropriate places in the book to do this. Also, on the 7th day, in the spaces provided, document the specific actions you will be taking to empower your life.

Repetition is the Mother of learning. Thus, there are certain critical concepts that are repeated, from different angles, in different Reflections. Take note of these instances for reinforcement of the concepts. Moreover, when you are conscious that a concept has been repeated, ask yourself whether you are observing the concept. If you are not observing it massively and effectively, commit to act on it.

The simple manner in which the book, *Reflective Empowerment*, is structured facilitates the release of a person's potential and greatness. You are asked to take only two actions: to read reflectively, and to take appropriate consistent action that will empower your success. Read, Reflect, and Review to Reveal Your Brilliance. You can be personally empowered, as you are the star of your own show. The choice is yours. Do it!

INTRODUCTION

Reflective Empowerment provides the backdrop to enable you to design the precise life you want—it details hw to empower yourself.

The fruits of empowering yourself are an abundant life, and your improved contribution to others, your environment and your community. The photographs illustrated in Reflective Empowerment depict some of the outcomes of empowering yourself.

Empowerment is the strength within you to be and do what you visualize. Empowerment is triggered when you have the freedom to do what makes you happy, and the power to get it done. With modern technology you are no longer isolated with limitations of communicating. You can now be connected to all human knowledge, and empowered by infinite possibilities. You empower yourself when you choose to design and control your life, rather than let apathy and complacency rule.

My life's journey of 84 years provided many diverse experiences for which I am grateful. My top passion is supporting people to bring out their potential and greatness. This thread of passion was evident in all I did from age 17. Whether it was in my activities of cricket, table tennis, karate, chess, or football. My professional training as a business economist, chartered secretary, banker, and chartered accountant also facilitated my having access to people to help them unleash their brilliance. Being a former chairman of a commercial bank, an international airline, and a national petroleum marketing company gave me the opportunity to interact with people in pursuit of my passion to support others to be the best that they could be.

After my formal retirement at age 60 from fulltime corporate life, I pursued the career of Lifestyle Coach to intensify my passion for the personal growth of others. This has been exciting.

It occurred to me that I could record some of my experiences for the benefit of others. This led to my authoring ten motivational books as follows:

- Live a Life of 'Virtual' Success (2003)
* The Executive Speaks (2005)
- Infinite Possibilities (2007)
- Glimpses of Greatness (2009)
- Reflective Empowerment (2010)
- From Humble Beginnings (2011)
- Enlightened Corporate Leadership (2013)
- Think, Be Still, & Grow Spiritually (2015)
- 10 Proven 21st Century Success Generators (2016)
- National Commercial Banking in Trinidad and Tobago (2017)

In my quest to support others to be empowered, between 2004 and 2010 I sent out a weekly e-newsletter to my list. The feedback from the readers was great. To extend the reach of these empowerment reflections, they have been collated, and designed into this book, *Reflective Empowerment.* May you read, enjoy, and be empowered.

Establish your true self

CHAPTER 1: LOOK WITHIN

1. You can transcend your despondency

Are you distressed, despondent, down-spirited, or depressed? Most persons experiencing such debility are not exploring their full potential. You become bored because you are not taking action consistent with the skill set and talents that you have. You make excuses for your condition, but you do not accept that it is your responsibility to change things. If you want things to change, you have to change. You cannot continue doing the things you have been doing for the past twelve months and expect to get a different outcome than your present situation. Choose to change your current game plan.

One approach is to decide on a goal beyond the narrow confines of yourself. If you have a goal that helps others, while providing you with personal fulfillment and/or income, then perhaps you will have something to wake up for in the morning. Each person will have a different calling. You must decide what are your gifts and talents, where there is a need, and your wholesome desire to act on the opportunity.

There is another approach you can take. Tomorrow morning when you awake, ask yourself, why am I alive today? Document what comes to you in response to that question. Repeat the exercise on your awaking for the next six days (seven days in all). As you follow this process, you will experience a deepening and better understanding of your purpose. You will also find that your life becomes more meaningful and fulfilled. Be relentless in the quest for your significance.

2. Believe beyond the present moment

Your success depends on the belief you have in yourself. You want something different in your life. You do not have it at the moment, but do you believe that you can attain it? Unless you believe that you can attain it, you will not. You have previous successes, and therefore you can have the confidence that you are up to achieving what you want in life. You learned to walk, talk, eat, and think. You passed exams, and you are doing many varied things each day. You have a history of success, and you can build on this expertise.

A setback in life is that you do not clearly and specifically determine what you want. For example, you may say that you want a house. That is not specific enough. You must determine, the size and cost of house, the possible areas where the house should be, and the time frame in which you want to occupy it. The more specific you can be, the more likely it will be achieved.

A second element to achieve what you want is that you must be passionate about it. Not warm, or cold, but hot. You must really love having it, and get joy and fulfillment from its attainment. Next, you must develop plans, and strategies to deliver it, including polishing your skill-set in relation to your desires.

Finally, you must take massive, consistent, relevant action to materialize your desires. Keep reviewing your progress, and make appropriate changes to your game plan where necessary.

You must believe in yourself to be the success that you want to be. Belief in oneself is half of the battle of achievement. Putting it another way, if you believe you can, you probably can. If you believe you cannot, you will prove yourself right. Belief is the self-starting switch that gets you off the launching pad. Believe in yourself and soar like an eagle!

3. Beyond hope

Hope is a necessary element in your success equation. Hope is the longing and wishing for something you do not have, but believe that having it will enhance your life. Hope is merely your intention that something of importance will happen in your life, but at the moment it is not clearly achievable. In fact, being alive always triggers the possibility to hope.

Anyway, be careful that you do not use the concept of hope as a conditioned belief that there is nothing that you can do, but sit back and hope for the best. This conditioned belief puts you in a powerless pattern, and stifles the vibrant action that you could otherwise take to manifest your intention of hope.

Hope is important as it raises your expectations of achievement, and what you expect you get. However, hope on its own is not enough. You have to go beyond hope to ACTION. This is akin to the admonition of, faith without works is dead. Hope without appropriate action is fantasy.

You can live in hope, and just wish and wait for things to happen.

Alternatively, you can go beyond the waiting game, and design strategies and plans that will take you nearer to realizing your hope.

So, what are you hoping for in your life? Review what is the most important thing you are HOPING for in your life. Consider whether you are taking serious relevant action to bring your most priority HOPE to fruition. If you are not developing serious action plans, then start to develop, and activate those plans. If you are already taking action on your cherished hope, double the effort, and be consistent in its pursuit. You will then gloriously enter your Door of Hope.

4. Building relationships

You are so different from other persons that you have a unique DNA. This means that to have a good and proper relationship with someone else requires a common platform where you can relate to each other with a common understanding. This is definitely not easy to do.

Despite individual uniqueness, there are some elements and core values that are common to most humans. Thus, if you can adopt them, there is a good chance that you can develop and improve any relationship. There are four areas of credibility that foster good relationships. These are:

- *Credibility with yourself.* Do you believe in who you are, and what you do. Then, others can believe in you, and trust you.
- *Credibility of your intent.* What is your intention in the relationship? Is it for your exclusive benefit, or is it for your mutual benefit?

- *Credibility of your capacity.* What is your capability, skills and talents in relation to what you are purporting to deliver?
- *Credibility of the results of your track record.* Your ability to get things done, and to make things happen.

There are certain behaviors of people who are highly trusted in relationships. Three of these key behaviors are:

- You must demonstrate concern for the other person
- You must deliver results consistently
- You must be your word, and keep your commitments rigorously— no excuses

Deepen these elements of behavior, and you will surely experience enhanced relationships.

5. Pain is a barometer for action

The world is so constructed that if you wish to enjoy its pleasures you must also endure its pains. You cannot have one without the other. To get to the mountain top, you have to pass through the valley of despair, and you have to endure and overcome the slope of the hill. To enjoy the beauty of the rose, you have to accept the threat of the thorn. You achieve to the extent that you overcome the negative. Achievers are willing to pay the price of achievement.

The battle of life requires continuous effort and sustained application: this translates to sacrifice and pain. If there were nothing to struggle for, there would be nothing to be achieved. If there were no difficulties or pain, there would be no success or achievement.

When you achieve anything you seldom really appreciate it, if it comes easily. If the prize is worthwhile, most times you have to sacrifice your time, relationships, energy and money. There are no gains without pains.

There is another aspect of pain; it alerts you to the fact that something is not quite right with the situation. This enables you to consider taking action to correct the imbalance.

Day 6 review

You have reflected for the past 5 days on different Inspirational Reflections in this book. You should now indicate what insights you got from your reading. List below at least 2 or 3 insights that you got from the Reflections, or information that was reinforced or confirmed.

_____

_____

_____

_____

Day 7 review

You have reflected for the past 6 days on different Inspirational Reflections. To get the best from the material, list below at least 2 areas or particular situations in your life in which you commit to do better.

_____

_____

_____

_____

6. Cherish and polish your gift of speech

One of your greatest gifts is that you are able to speak. This permits you to let others know how you think, feel, and the vision you have for your life. You use speech to convey your innermost feelings, your core values, your expectations, and your hurts.

The tragedy is that since you were speaking from about age 2, and you have made your way reasonably well in the world, you may think that you do not need to polish your speaking skills. Yes, you can take your gift of speech to a higher level. You can polish the speaking gem that you already have. It will improve the chances of your being more successful. If you understand some of the elements of effective speaking, you can enhance the power of your messages on a daily basis every time you speak.

A convenient method to enhance your presentation skills is to pursue a training program in public speaking, or join a Dale Carnegie Course or become a member of a Toastmasters International Club.

7. Five Pillars of Commitment for your success

Your commitment should be to keep doing what you agreed with yourself, and with others to do, despite your reluctance, and strong feeling not to continue to do it. Success is the result of making and keeping commitments with yourself, and others. The 5 Pillars of Commitment for your success are:

- Continuous life long learning
- Follow your dreams powerfully, and without reserve
- Do your best always, although it might mean leaving your comfort zone
- Pursue a life of love, and kindness
- Persevere with your will to win and succeed

There are also 4 Agreements of Life that you should make with yourself to power and guide your success. These agreements are:

- Do not make assumptions. Enquire and clarify what the situation is. Do not believe that you can read the other person's mind. Often you will be wrong, and making assumptions destroy relationships.
- Do not take things personally. Most times what a person says or does is a reflection of the baggage the person is carrying. People's wrong opinion of you should not become your reality.
- Always be your word. Whatever you say, honor it, and to do this you must be careful, in the first place, with what you say
- Give your best efforts at all times. No one can blame you if you have given your all.

You design your future by what you do from moment to moment. Thus, every moment is precious and valuable; so invest in your life moment by moment through following the 5 Pillars of Commitment, and the 4 Agreements of Life.

You have the power to be your best by starting each day with speed of action, continuing the momentum during the day, and finishing the day with strong commitment. You have the talent within to shine brightly in your life. Release your brilliance. You can do it.

8. Mistakes are necessary for success

The only person who does not make a mistake is the person who does nothing. You will not make a mistake, if you do nothing, or very little.

The reverse of this is, that the more activity you engage in, the greater the chance that you will make mistakes.

Most successful people are into massive activity—activity—activity—activity. Certainly mistakes will be made, but the more mistakes, the greater the success. Take risks without being reckless. You have a center of balance that will guide you to be prudent. This can be a watershed moment to point you to your new mountain of achievement. It is up to you to put into practice all the wisdom you have been exposed to over the years.

Decide, clarify, plan, act, and review, and your dream will come true. But remember that every dream carries with it, a responsibility to act on that dream to manifest it. You can do it. Dream, act, and achieve!

9. Transcend wrong opinions others have of you

One of my close friends, Ray, was very distressed. A family member he cherished said something quite awful about Ray's behavior. Ray was distressed. I told him not to worry, but just ignore the comment, and don't accept the invalid opinion. How could I do that? Ray questioned.

I knew that Ray did not eat pork, as he considered it unhealthy. I asked Ray, if he were given a beautiful pork ham whether he would accept it? Quite predictably Ray said no. I then asked him who would then own the ham? He replied, the original owner of course. Well I said, when someone comments wrongfully about you, merely do not accept it. The invalid comment will then remain with the person making the comment. Transcend the invalid comment, and do not make it your reality.

You must not make a wrong opinion another person has of you become your reality. You have the power to determine what you will let enter your consciousness. One clue is to understand that if you are obsessed with what others think about you—your reputation—you will be in great turmoil. You have to know who you are, what you stand for, do what is just and right, and then be indifferent to the wrong opinions others may have of you. Stand in the power of the knowledge you have of yourself. No one knows your qualities better than you. Stand in your light.

10. Think and plan instead of worrying

Why should you worry that something may happen? Worry cannot solve an impending danger. Ask yourself: can I do anything about the matter? If you can make no difference to the situation, your worrying is pointless. If you believe you can make a difference to the outcome of what you are concerned about, then you need to do some thinking about it—advance thinking and not advance worrying.

When you think about the matter as opposed to worrying about it, you begin to see the possibilities. When you think through the possibilities, and determine what choices you will make in the matter, you can then plan for the outcome you desire.

Anticipation is one of the signs of true wisdom You gain the advantage by doing things before they need to be done. Position yourself ahead of time, like the goalkeeper who anticipates where the striker is likely to place the ball, and then positions himself in goal before the player shoots the ball. Don't worry and be in a flurry. Rather think, plan and achieve.

Day 6 review

You have reflected for the past 5 days on different Inspirational Reflections in this book. You should now indicate what insights you got from your reading. List below at least 2 or 3 insights that you got from the Reflections, or information that was reinforced or confirmed.

_____

_____

_____

_____

Day 7 review

You have reflected for the past 6 days on different Inspirational Reflections. To get the best from the material, list below at least 2 areas or particular situations in your life in which you commit to do better.

_____

_____

_____

_____

11. The best and worst of life

The story goes that an Emperor commanded his wise men to roam the world, and return to him when one of them learned the secret of life—the best and worst of it. In due season one of them returned with the answer. When questioned, in answer to what was the best thing in life, the wise courtier stuck out his tongue. The Emperor was puzzled, but he put the next question of what was the worst thing in life? In reply, the wise courtier stuck out his tongue again.

The Emperor was annoyed, and asked for a good explanation, or death would be the wise courtier's reward. The wise one explained that with your tongue you could be loving, kind, supportive, compassionate, inspirational, teach others spiritual truths, praise your Maker, and speak a healing word, among many other positive interactions. The wise courtier quickly added that your tongue could also be used in quite the opposite way. It could be used to curse, lie, defame, malign, libel, blaspheme, deceive, and produce many other negative energies.

The Emperor reflected on something he had read in the Holy Scriptures that, ***Death and life are in the power of the tongue,,,*** Proverbs 18:21.

What then is the lesson to be learned from this episode dear Champion? You need to be extremely conscious of what you do with your tongue from moment to moment. In fact, the admonition in Psalm 141:3 can be very instructive for your personal growth, as it thunders, ***Set a watch O Lord before my mouth; keep the door of my lips.***

12. Build your self-confidence

Do you know that your mental, spiritual, and financial resources are foundational to achieve what you want? You have what it takes to be the success that you want to be. You have been endowed with internal skills that generate the resources—financial, creative and otherwise. However, you must claim it. You need to accept that you have what it takes. You have to be self-confident; secure in the knowledge that you can, but not be arrogant.

Your greatest weapon is your mind. What the mind can conceive, truly believe, and act upon can be achieved. The question of your self-confidence surfaces again. Do remember that your mind is so constructed that it will not generate a thought in you that cannot be manifested by you. Accept your internal wisdom, and be resolute in your actions.

The research has shown that by the time a person attains the age of 8, he/she has been given so many negatives—no, no, do not do this, and do not do that—the self-esteem and self-confidence of that person are shattered. Parents and guardians spoke these negative admonitions out of love, for the children's protection. What they did not know was that every time the child was told a negative, there needed to be eight positive statements to counteract that one negative.

The good news is that as an adult, you now have the option to bombard your mind with positive thoughts to build your self-confidence.

Continue that positive pathway with great intentionality, and that will give you another piece of the puzzle of life.

In the next reflection, another piece of the puzzle of self-empowerment will be presented. In the meanwhile, work on improving your self-confidence!

13. The gap in your life must be purposeful

Life consists of three main parts: your birth, your death, and the gap between these two events. The way you live in the gap is the whole purpose of life. If you consider the sequence of the evolution of a baby, you will notice that it grows, learns, and is joyful. Similarly, your purpose is to grow, to learn, and to be happy, joyful, and fulfilled.

Life is very diversified, with many distractions, disappointments, and despair. But life is also full of opportunities, possibilities, and golden moments. You can have as your compass for living four elements to guide you. These are Discipline, Attitude, Success, and Happiness.

Life is controlled by the discipline you exercise. Discipline is doing what needs to be done, when it needs to done, although you do not feel like doing it. What NEEDS to be done, not what you WANT to do. Also, if you are guided by feelings, the negativity in the world will distract you.

Your attitude determines what you will accomplish. There are different aspects of attitude, but focus on the attitude of gratitude. Be thankful for what you have, and do not dwell on what is missing

Philip Guy Rochford

in your life. What you put your attention on grows stronger in your life. Continuously develop an attitude of gratitude.

Success has many definitions. A simple one is achieving what you earnestly desire. This success principle covers both spiritual and material things. To be a success, you must clarify what it is you really want, and go after it assiduously. The target of your success must bring you peace, joy, and happiness, if it is to have significant meaning for you.

Happiness comes from using your potential, and involves using your powers in excellence to their greatest extent. Another take on it is, that happiness arises when you use your talents in the service of others. In short, happiness occurs when you use your potential to manifest the potential of others. Combine these elements of Discipline, Attitude, Success and Happiness to the fullest, and you will soar like an eagle, and be the best that you can be.

14. Upgrade your belief system

Many people are operating below their full potential. Are you one of them? You have the power and ability to ignite your passion, and activate your hidden brilliance. Your thoughts, words, and actions arise from the various beliefs you have on particular matters. In fact, you have a belief about almost everything, although very often, it is quite unconscious. Thus, if you are experiencing limitation, struggle, or hardship in any area of your life, there is a belief in that area that does not serve your intentions in life. You have to clarify, change, clear, and contradict that non-serving belief.

20

Improve your chances of success, by strengthening the three pillars of thinking, focusing, and action steps. What are you thinking about continuously grows stronger in your life. Be careful about criticizing, condemning, and complaining about others and situations. Most importantly, do not criticize, condemn or complain about yourself.

What you focus on is what will get done because of your systematic attention. However, be sensitive to the moment, and the opportunities that unexpectedly present themselves. Being flexible, without compromising your principles, confronts reality, and optimizes opportunity.

A critical aspect of moving towards a more successful life is to take different action. If you want to move beyond where you are at present, you have to take some different action to what you have been doing in the last nine to twelve months. The same thinking, focus and action that brought you to your present level of success, cannot take you to the next higher level of success.

Sameness is the enemy of growth. What this means is that you have a real challenge to move out of your comfort zone. If you want to progress, you have to do better than you are doing now, and this requires you to make more diligent efforts than you are making at present. You can rise to your next higher level of performance. Believe in yourself, and in your potential.

15. Use mistakes as stepping-stones to success

The only person who does not make a mistake is a person who does nothing. As long as you are doing something, taking some action, being involved in some activity, you must make a mistake. You are human.

You are not perfect. You do not have all the answers. You are fallible.

When you understand your humanity, you can make use of mistakes.

A mistake is an opportunity for you to learn what to avoid or what to do to achieve your goal. When the inventor of the light bulb, Thomas Edison, tried 999 to produce light and did not succeed, he persisted and on the next try he found the solution to produce light. When his friends asked him how it felt to fail 999 times, and did such failure not discourage him, the inventor responded by pointing out that he found 999 ways in which light was not produced. He saw the mistakes that prevented light from being created as stepping stones to success. Failure is only a bad thing when you stop trying because of it.

The greater your success, the greater number of mistakes you have usually made in relation to the non-achievers. If you have passion for what you are doing, and the courage to keep on trying despite ostensible failure, great will be your reward.

Day 6 review

You have reflected for the past 5 days on different Inspirational Reflections in this book. You should now indicate what insights you got from your reading. List below at least 2 or 3 insights that you got from the Reflections, or information that was reinforced or confirmed.

_____

_____

_____

_____

Day 7 review

You have reflected for the past 6 days on different Inspirational Reflections. To get the best from the material, list below at least 2 areas or particular situations in your life in which you commit to do better.

_____

_____

_____

_____

16. Learn from losing

In life you experience both success and failure. When you fail or lose, it simply means that you did not get what you wanted. Your attitude towards so called failure should be that you can learn something useful from the process of disappointment.

Every experience of success or failure has a lesson waiting to be learned. Learn the lesson from every experience. Losing is never fun. It hurts in so many different ways, especially when it's something that you were really looking forward to, or something that you were passionately involved in, or something that you wanted badly.

I recall in my mid 20s I was denied the opportunity to be appointed a Management Cadet Prison Officer, although I had topped the list of applicants at the interview. I was really disappointed, and resentful of the Senior Administrative Officer who advised that it was a waste of my talents to be placed in Prison Administration. How dare him to determine what was good for me. It meant dashing my plans to become an attorney-at-law.

However, learning from the experience, I went on to obtain a scholarship to study in the United Kingdom for a degree in business economics, finishing up being a chartered secretary, and a chartered accountant. Eventually, I retired as chairman and managing director of a commercial bank.

Instead of having your negative monologues, you have the opportunity to take time to **reflect**, **rethink**, **recollect** or **re-group** on what to do differently for your future success. Follow this process, and you are guaranteed to come out swinging harder and better the next time. You have everything to gain by examining the seeds of disappointment, to learn the success story that they embody. Press on, and learn.

17. Did you take action for success last week?

What action have you taken on the previous reflections? Merely absorbing information without acting on it is wasteful, does nothing to bring the best out of you, and does not support living your dreams powerfully.

To be successful, you must take positive action on a daily basis. How have you done in the last seven days? Consider how many days you actually followed the action process, and took goal-oriented action. Step up your activities, and you will release your hidden talent. You can do it.

Consider this concept. You now have the possibility to generate energy to take action in the next three months to fulfill your dreams. Simply follow the one percent (1%) success principle: this requires you every day for the next ninety days to take at least two action steps in pursuit of one or both of your two highest priority goals for the next 1twelve months. The emphasis is on ACTION STEPS, as opposed to thinking, dreaming, speaking, or merely writing about them. GO FOR IT.

18. Act now for your progress or success

Your progress or success relies on proper timing, and speed of action. People in the world who make things happen, value and share a sense of urgency in doing what strikes them as needed to be done.

You can step up to better performance in your life by acting timely on your urges and desires. Acting with alacrity will provide results that astound you. No matter how intelligent or capable you are, if you do not have a sense of urgency (not impatience) you will not blossom as beautifully as you are capable of becoming.

You can embrace, or deepen, from today a philosophy of, DO IT NOW. This new attitude will change your life dramatically in a positive way, and the time to start is NOW.

Create a massive sense of urgency in all the key things you need to do. Do not delay. To start following your new DO IT NOW philosophy, consider three (3) important things that you have been intending to do, but you have not done them. Pick important activities that you have been thinking and tinkering about, and commit to start them today with a mind-set to finish them.

Get started to become the masterful person that is inside of you. Embrace the DO IT NOW philosophy, as to delay is to decay.

Your progress or success is linked directly to your goals. Settle on your goals program, and this will be your guide to support you in taking action at the appropriate urgent time. You must take action when it needs to be taken, where it needs to be taken, although you may not feel like taking it. Follow the whispers of your heart, do it now, and you will release the greatness that is in you.

19. What is your story?

One of my international coaches, Mike Litman, sent me a DVD of a week-end workshop he held for Lifestyle Coaches in the USA. He enquired of them whether they had been sharing their stories, as this keeps the attention of their markets. This led me to think of my own story, and the system I used for my success. The system I used for success is outlined in my e-books, Live a Life of Virtual Success, and Glimpses of Greatness (my autobiography) and they can be purchased on the internet.

Part of my story after the age of normal retirement, is shared in my co-authored book, A search for Purpose, and states in part as follows.

In 1993 at the age of sixty, I retired from the National Commercial Bank as Chairman and Managing Director. My new career of Lifestyle Coach was building people directly, rather than focus on growth and transformation of institutions. The Lifestyle Coaching Industry had not yet penetrated Trinidad and Tobago. I pioneered this growth opportunity. My experience of relatedness in life and careers, naturally supported a lifestyle coaching methodology.

This led me to understand that one of my roles was to be *"my brother's keeper."* Since then, this spiritual precept has been my primary guiding light. It is the foundation for all my success.

Take action now to document your story, and grasp new insights this reflection unfolds for you.

You can step up the success that is possible in your life. Dream big dreams. Dreams are what strengthens the belief in yourself, and permits you to say, I can, I will, and I must.

Take action now to review the success system I used as outlined in my e-book, Live a Life of Virtual Success.

20. Risk failure to get a chance of succeeding

A Chief Executive Officer of one of Fortune's top 100 successful companies was once asked by a young executive for a formula for success. The CEO's reply was "double your failure rate." The law of averages provides that the more you fail, the greater your chance of succeeding. Failure is often an important necessary step in achieving success. If you don't take the risk of failing, you won't get the chance to succeed. One Sage put it this way, " You have not tasted success until you have tasted failure."

If you have never failed at anything, you are operating at far below your potential. You are not stretching yourself. You are not taking any risk of failure. If you are afraid to lose, you cannot challenge yourself and others who compete with you. To be the winner that you are capable of being, you must be willing to experience "so called failure." Remember that failure works for you, if you can learn from your mistakes. So, do not be afraid to fail your way to success.

Day 6 review

   You have reflected for the past 5 days on different Inspirational Reflections in this book. You should now indicate what insights you got from your reading. List below at least 2 or 3 insights that you got from the Reflections, or information that was reinforced or confirmed.

_____

_____

_____

_____

Day 7 review

You have reflected for the past 6 days on different Inspirational Reflections. To get the best from the material, list below at least 2 areas or particular situations in your life in which you commit to do better.

_____

_____

_____

21. Relieve your stress

Life is complex, with distractions, challenges and opportunities. This leads to all of us having some form of stress from time to time. Stress is simply your emotional response to what occurs in your life. It is a natural part of living, but you can combat it, if you want to. Stress manifests as continuous noise in your head. You entertain myriads of thoughts, and they keep circulating in your mind continuously.

Repetition is a proven technique for instilling a habit. Follow for 30 days this structured technique for 5 minutes twice per day, at about 6.00 AM and 6.00 PM, and you will be on your way to improved effectiveness in your life.

Sit comfortably in a straight back chair with your back and spine in an upright position perpendicular to the floor. (or sit in a lotus position with an erect back and spine posture). Get into a relaxed frame of mind. The soles of your feet should be on the floor (if you are not in a lotus position) and your hands uncrossed. Close your eyes, take three deep breaths, and then breathe normally:

(1) Observe your breathing. Simply observe without taking any action to change your breathing.
(2) Become aware of the space your body occupies, but continue observing your breathing.
(3) Be conscious of the chair you are sitting on.
(4) Be conscious of where your feet meet the floor.

(5) Be conscious of the upright posture of your back, all the time observing the rhythm of your breathing.

(6) Be aware of the air passing through your nostrils, as you breathe in, and you breathe out.

(7) During this breathing process, thoughts will arise. Do not fight these thoughts, but merely gently, and innocently put your attention back on observing your breathing.

Thoughts arising, is one of the means by which your body throws off stress. However, do not follow the thoughts. Gently and innocently put your attention back on the rhythm of your breathing. Continue the focus on observing the rhythm of your breathing, and end the exercise in 5 minutes.

At the end of the exercise sit quietly for 15 seconds, and then open your eyes slowly and gently. You will now be feeling relaxed, strengthened your ability to focus, combated your stress, and be ready to take on the challenges that confront you.. Remember to do this exercise twice every day for 30 consecutive days.

22. Continue the year with strong success

If you have been diligently following the process laid out in this book of reflections, just over one month would have elapsed. Thus, it is time to reflect on, and review what you have done so far. On assessment, you may find that you have not accomplished as much as you intended. However, this can be corrected by taking stronger action in the next ninety days.

You will notice that some of the roadblocks that prevented your success were as follows:

- There was considerable discomfort and inconvenience due to the many sacrifices you were required to make.
- Following your natural likes and dislikes, and being guided by your natural preferences and prejudices, did not energize you to successful action.
- Staying within your comfort zone, not being prepared to take acceptable risks, and postponing decisions and actions, prevented your forward thrust.

You now have the possibility to generate energy to take action in the next three months to fulfill your dreams for the current year. Simply follow the one percent success principle: this requires you every day for the next ninety days to take at least two action steps in pursuit of one or both of your two highest priority goals for this year.

The emphasis is on ACTION STEPS, as opposed to thinking, dreaming, speaking, or merely writing about them.

Be consistent and persistent in following this one percent success principle for the next three months, and you will reap untold benefits in your life. You can do it. Step up to your own responsibility and accountability.

23. The power of forgiveness

Your mind is powerful. Your mind stores, and can recall events that occurred many years ago. You have the choice to harbor or release events that you have experienced. When someone says or does something that hurts you, it is usually difficult to think kindly of that person. You can dwell on the hurt, or you can release it.

How do you let go of this horrible hurt? This can be your golden moment of decision to tap into the POWER OF FORGIVENESS. You can decide at this very moment to release your baggage of past hurts. Forgiveness releases the putrid energy that you have stored within yourself. Forgiveness does not give a benefit to the person who hurt you. It releases the mental clouds that distort your own power to rise to your best self.

A heavy iron ball attached to your leg can represent a past hurt. When you forgive someone who has hurt you, the iron ball that it represents is released, and the act of forgiving the person gives you freedom from a heavy burden. Thus, to forgive benefits you, rather than the person being forgiven.

Forgive your mother, father, guardian, brother, sister, cousin, close friend, acquaintance, boss, co-worker, or whoever hurt you in the past. You need to do this to stop hurting yourself. Drop the pain of past wounds, to be able to focus on being the best that you can be.

The spiritual concept is what you sow you will reap. If you do not forgive others, your own errors will not be forgiven. Remember that part of the Lord's Prayer that states, " .... forgive us our trespasses as we forgive those that trespass against us ...." Moreover, forgiveness and release are important aspects of love.

When you tap into the power of forgiveness, you will unleash your undoubted greatness. Make mental room for the gifts that the Universe wants to unfold to you. Make room for the best days ahead of you by releasing the pain of past hurts, through the power of forgiveness. You can do it. Just decide and be intentional!

24. Honor your commitments

The extent to which you honor your commitments, is the extent to which you generate your success. You either keep your commitments to yourself and to others, or you do not keep them. When you do not keep your commitments, forget about the excuses. You simply have sabotaged your success. Failure to honor one commitment does not mean that you will not be successful, but the habit of not keeping commitments will certainly lead to non-achievement of your goals.

If you make a commitment, honor it. If you make a promise, keep it. If you set a goal achieve it. Success results from making and keeping commitments to yourself and others. Goals, projects and relationships that fail are the direct result of broken commitments. It's that simple, that profound, and that important. A commitment made, must be honored, as each one is ultimately interconnected with your success.

The power of your commitment to success suggests that you should only give your word or commitment when it is important to give, and has meaning in its accomplishment. Thus, do not give your word merely to get rid of the moment. For example, telling someone you will telephone or call him/her with no commitment, or intention to really do it.

How great is the power of your commitments? Remember that your ability to honor your commitments directly impacts your credibility, reputation, trustworthiness, earning ability, and overall peace of mind.

You are simply one person, but you can still make a difference in this world. You cannot do everything, but you can do anything you put your mind to do with passion and consistency

Start the day right with vision and focus, and finish the day strong, having honored your commitments. Be the success that you are capable of being.

25. Power of your mind

Your mind is a powerful instrument. The mind sets the limits to what you can do. It overrides your potential. If in fact you can do something, but your mind says to you that you cannot do it, then the reality is you will not be able to do it.

The Great Prophet once said "if you have faith as small as a mustard seed, you will tell the mountain to remove and it will move." Each person has a special ability to look at a situation and to know whether it is possible to deal with that situation. You have to believe in yourself.

You have to reach deep within your soul, feel that you can do the job at hand, and then through your thoughts make the world that you want. Belief is the inner feeling that you can accomplish whatever you undertake. At another level, belief is what you consider to be true for any particular set of circumstances, or specific situations. With positive and creative thinking your opportunities can be grasped, and be materialized.

Day 6 review

You have reflected for the past 5 days on different Inspirational Reflections in this book. You should now indicate what insights you got from your reading. List below at least 2 or 3 insights that you got from the Reflections, or information that was reinforced or confirmed.

_____

_____

_____

_____

Day 7 review

You have reflected for the past 6 days on different Inspirational Reflections. To get the best from the material, list below at least 2 areas or particular situations in your life in which you commit to do better.

_____

_____

_____

_____

26. How serious are you about your success

In the midst of life, there is death. The death of Michael Jackson at age 50 reminded us of this. The world was presented with the greatness of Michael Jackson through the media, for at least 48 hours after his sudden death. What an outpouring of his acknowledgment.

As I looked at his several performances on the television and on the web, something struck me like a bolt of lightening. While from an early age it is clear that he had raw talent, that innate ability was nurtured, developed, and sustained through rigorous PREPARATION. Michael alluded to this when he said how sad he was that he could not go out to play in the Park as other children did, since he was required to practice, and prepare his craft. The superb dance performances could not be executed by Michael had he not had massive preparation. Proper Preparation Prevents Poor Performance—the 5Ps of excellence.

I reflected on my own life, and concluded that perhaps I could have accomplished more had I nurtured my inborn talents through greater preparation. I have decided to put greater effort and preparation in the use of my talents. What about you? Are you working your talents as assiduously as you could? You alone can answer that question. It is not too late to take some corrective action. Remember that the measure of your success is a function of your PREPARATION.

Michael Jackson was not perfect. Not one of us is perfect. One lesson to be learnt from the death of Michael Jackson is that life is to be lived, making full use of your unique talents for the benefit of others. Resolve today to do a little more to polish your talents. Prepare for your brilliance to shine more, by giving quality PREPARATION time to manifest your greatness. You have a contribution to make to society in your own special way. Honor it.

27. Be empowered and awakened

Thinking form habits, and habits design your life. A good habit is to end each day a better person than when you awoke that day. How would this be possible? During your waking hours, listen to something new, read something new, do something uplifting, say something inspirational to someone

By following this new daily design, you will be establishing *a habit of growth.* All that is required is for you to improve yourself by 1% each day. This is an achievable task. But imagine what 1%daily growth will do for you in one year's time—phenomenal growth. You can achieve whatever you really set your mind to do. You are the architect of your future. You are the star of your show. However, you have to show up. You have to take the action that is required to deliver your vision. You can do it.

Put your mind and energy to what you are passionate about: this will deliver the life you want for yourself. Be empowered, and be awakened through daily good habits. Develop the habit of doing something new and uplifting each day. Yes! You can do it!

28. Keep your journal of gratitude

Have you ever started something, and did not finish it? Most of us have experienced this. Perhaps you can conduct an experiment to combat this, and at the same time deepen your inner strength of appreciating the positives in your life. I am suggesting that you keep a Journal of Gratitude for thirty consecutive days. A notebook, or copybook will do, or use your computer, if you are so inclined. Thirty consecutive days is suggested, as research shows this period will increase the chances of the habit becoming ingrained in your consciousness. It will strengthen your inner exploration.

Expressions of gratitude unlock the fullness of your life. It increases what you already have. It shines a light of clarity in your life. Gratitude helps you to understand your past, and creates a new sense of hope for tomorrow.

The concept is simple. You are trained from birth to look for what's missing, and not what you have. The logical outcome is that you want more and more. In fact, that's what success is all about. I am inviting you to deliberately focus on an attitude of gratitude. This will generate more of what you want in your life. There is an ancient spiritual law that says, the more you are grateful for what you have, the more abundance will flow into your life.

The process of keeping the journal is that every day for thirty consecutive days, you record what you are grateful for in your life. It may be something special that occurred that day, or your health, your relationships, your spiritual consciousness, your career, or whatever you believe makes your life worthwhile. Be as specific as possible. The more specific you are, the more terrific you will become.

Target each day to record at least five things for which you are thankful. Do not repeat the same thing a second time within the thirty days. Look for a new thanksgiving each day.

Avoid the temptation to keep repeating the same things each day. Look for the silver lining in what is taking place with different situations each day. This positive expectancy will generate new possibilities in your life, and will open up creative opportunities for you. Give yourself this gift for the next thirty consecutive days. Go for it. You can do it.

29. Shift to a different and better life

Make your life for the next twelve months better than the last 12 months by doing things differently. If you continue to do exactly what you have been doing before, you will continue to get the same result that you wish to change. Change how you use and prioritize your time. Change the people you spend time with: add persons with a positive mind-set to your social network. Change your thoughts to see positive possibilities: say to yourself, yes this can be done and I will find a way, rather than it will not work.

One of the most important things in life is having a goal. The quality of the goal will determine the quality of your life. The most important aspect of a goal is having one. A GOAL is simply something you want to achieve. You achieve your goal by having a plan, strategy, tactics, and action. A PLAN is a simple road map of achieving that goal. STRATEGY is the overall game with the big steps. TACTICS are the baby steps you have to take to achieve strategy. ACTION is the energy that materializes the goal.

You must take massive, consistent, relevant action for your plans to materialize. Just take one action step at a time with focused determination, and the ensuing year will be your best year in life so far.

These two action exercises will help to develop a different and better life for you:

(1) Establish a weekly review time and day, and stick to that schedule every week. If it is 8.00 p.m. on a Sunday, stick to the schedule every week. It may be Friday at 5.00 p.m. or some other day and time. Decide on the weekly time and day, and faithfully keep your same review time every week. When you review, you will assess whether you are on track with your plan, and provide adjustments to make it a success.

(2) At least twice each day, ask yourself whether what you are then doing is the most productive way to spend your time. That is, will your activity at that moment help to further you along the way to achieve the plan you have for your life. If the activity is not supporting your dreams, change it. If the activity is in furtherance of achieving what you want in life, then soldier on. Continue the activity bravely.

May you dream big, but produce big actions as well. You can make your life better. Honor this commitment. You can do it.

30. Choices you make today shape your future

Your right to choose provides you with the key to unlock any door you dare to want to enter. You can decide where you are going to be, what you are going to do, and what you choose to think. No one can take away your power to choose.

You choose your attitude to life. You choose your core values. You need to have relevant and quality information in order to make sensible choices. You thus have a choice to be reliably informed. You can choose to update your knowledge continuously, and create a better universe for yourself. You can choose your friends and associates. You choose whether you have around you persons who will help you with your personal growth, or persons who will not support you to live your dreams powerfully.

Who you are today is as a result of your choices of yesterday. Who you will be tomorrow or what you will achieve in 5 years will depend on the choices you make currently from moment to moment. Deliberately choose wisely.

Day 6 review

You have reflected for the past 5 days on different Inspirational Reflections in this book. You should now indicate what insights you got from your reading. List below at least 2 or 3 insights that you got from the Reflections, or information that was reinforced or confirmed.

_____

_____

_____

_____

Day 7 review

You have reflected for the past 6 days on different Inspirational Reflections. To get the best from the material, list below at least 2 areas or particular situations in your life in which you commit to do better.

_____

_____

_____

_____

Let your vision be focused

31. Nurture your unique talents

You undoubtedly admire international and national icons. They exude positive energy. However, each icon is special, but cannot excel in all fields. For example, Roger Federer, male tennis champion, cannot excel in boxing. Tiger Woods, golf master, cannot excel in cricket. Brian Lara, world cricket champion cannot excel in football. Serena Williams, ladies tennis champion, cannot excel in ice-skating. Hasley Crawford, Trinidad and Tobago's first Olympic Gold Medalist, cannot excel in football. President Barack Obama, the great politician, cannot excel in baseball. The common factor is that each icon nurtured and developed his or her special skill.

What about you? What is your special skill or talent? How serious are you about developing that gift you have been given. Each of us has a special part to play in the design of the Universe. Ensure that you play your part well. Reflect and identify the area that people praise you for most. Resolve to develop your gift to its fullest. What you have to contribute to society is important. Every piece of the puzzle of life is important to the final solution. Your contribution is important. Raise your stakes. Act with courage and thoroughness. Your unique contribution may not appear important, but it is. A little salt may not appear important but it makes all the difference to the final taste of the food. So too is your contribution to society.

You may ask what can I contribute? Your contribution is to develop fully whatever you are best at doing. It may be your career, family, sports, spirituality, caring for others, or whatever it is that you excel in. Step up to the plate. Believe in yourself. Know that you have untold unused potential. Awake and let your brilliance shine. Polish the diamond that is within you. You can do it. Think your uplifting thoughts, and act with intentionality to achieve your dreams, while fulfilling your life's destiny.

32. Re-visit your goals

You have been designed to have desires. From babyhood you have had various desires; there was the desire for food, warmth, and play. As you grew, these desires took different forms, and as you became more adult, your desires were converted to goals. You had desires that could not be achieved at the moment, but you set a goal to achieve them.

A goal is a predetermined target or objective that you want to achieve. Some examples are: to increase your income to a certain amount, to buy a car, to own a home, to go on a vacation, and to get married. You set goals everyday, either consciously or unconsciously. Put simply, when you have a target, you are more likely to aim and hit it, as opposed to firing aimlessly without focus. However, if you wish to be successful in achieving what you want, there is a system of goal setting that you should follow.

The purpose of goals is to focus your attention, and provide a system to counteract diversions and distractions that take you away from pursuing your purpose. Re-visit and review how you are tapping into your desires through your goal setting program.

33. Reach for greater success.

You are a person with both material and spiritual attributes. Thus, you need to grow in both areas. If you want greater success in your life, follow this three-step process:

First

Decide very clearly what you want. This must be a core desire—something that goes to the seat of your passion. Something that gives meaning to your life.

Second

Find someone who has achieved what you want to achieve, and adopt this person as your mentor. You need not meet a mentor in person, nor even speak to that person, although both are desirable. You merely have to read and view what that person advises through audios, DVDs and books, and then implement the advice. You can also connect with someone who knows the mentor personally, or has been himself/herself coached by the mentor.

Third

Follow through with resolute action, and be consistent and persistent. This is an important part of the puzzle of success.

In a subsequent Reflection, you will get another piece of the success puzzle. *Until then, to your greater success!!*

34. Release your brilliance

You have a spark of Divinity in you that shines from time to time. This is responsible for your achievements to date. You have accomplished many things in your life, but you can accomplish even more. Your brilliance is hidden, but it can be released. However, the brilliant insight is not by itself achievement. Insights become effective through hard systematic work.

What then can you do to release your hidden brilliance? Follow these steps and you will achieve a positive difference in your life:

- Accept and truly believe that you can do more than you are doing at present. Research shows that you use only 5% of your brain power.
- Identify something that you are passionate about, that also benefits others, and proceed to pursue it relentlessly. When you help others to get what they want, you get what you want.
- Every day for the next 30 days eliminate, for 15 minutes, an activity that does not support the lifestyle you desire. Every minute wasted in a day is lost forever, so minimize wasted minutes.
- Every day for the next 30 days, for 30 minutes, read, listen to, or view some form of motivational material. What gets into your mind affects your persona. Ensure that your mind is bombarded with sufficient positive thoughts to balance off all the environmental negativity.
- At the end of 30 days review your progress, and establish new action plans that will materialize your desires. A life worth living is a life worth reviewing. Inspect and detect what actions are worthy for your pursuit.

You have the power to live the life you want. However, you must want it badly enough, and recognize the benefits you will derive. Whether you achieve your dreams will depend on the choices you make day in and day out. Choose wisely and let your brilliance shine brightly. Rise to your full potential. You can do it.

35. Your actions mirror your thoughts

There is the inner kingdom and the outer kingdom. This may also be expressed as the spiritual kingdom and the physical kingdom. From the point of view of the individual, the internal kingdom can be seen as inner thoughts, mental observations or intellectual positioning. The outer kingdom is expressed by the actions taken by the individual, and the results that occur in the individual's life on a day-to-day basis.

How you think shows up in how you act. As you think in your heart, you usually act on the outer. Your attitudes and actions mirror your mind. They reflect your thinking. People can know what you are thinking by looking at what you are doing. Actions mirror thoughts. The thoughts you have chosen in the past account for your state in the world today. Your actions are the best interpreters of your thoughts. What goes on inside of you is eventually reflected in your outer actions.

Thus, your challenge is to have thoughts that support your core values, thoughts that mirror your positive expectations, and benevolent thoughts towards others. And most importantly, eliminate negative thoughts about yourself. Have thoughts about yourself that lift your self-confidence and self-esteem, as you are a wonderful expression of Creation.

Day 6 review

You have reflected for the past 5 days on different Inspirational Reflections in this book. You should now indicate what insights you got from your reading. List below at least 2 or 3 insights that you got from the Reflections, or information that was reinforced or confirmed.

_____

_____

_____

_____

Day 7 review

You have reflected for the past 6 days on different Inspirational Reflections. To get the best from the material, list below at least 2 areas or particular situations in your life in which you commit to do better.

_____

_____

_____

36. Rise to the world economic challenge

The world, from time to time, spins through cyclical economic decline. What does this mean for you? Each person's situation is different, but there are some basic stances that you can take to ride the rough waves of international economic decline.

First, know and believe that you have what it takes to survive. You have a keen intellect, and you can cultivate a positive expectancy. Second, change in your life is ever present. You can develop an attitude to see an opportunity in every changing challenge. Third, by achieving what you have so far in life, establishes your history of success. Building on this experience can ensure your continued success. Fourth and not least, you have to assess and analyze your income streams, and your expenses.

You need to increase your income streams, or generate them more efficiently. You will also need to eliminate or reduce expenditure that is not absolutely necessary. For instance, reducing the time spent on lengthy unnecessary social telephone calls.

You can optimize your expenses by substituting cheaper products for more expensive ones. Examples are substituting raw peanuts that you parch in the oven, for bottled nuts; and plain biscuits and jam for more expensive and sophisticated packaged cream biscuits. Of course, this is only for a season, to take account of declining economic buoyancy.

Be confident that you have enough experience and creativity to master the changing economic scenery. Go forward with confidence in your future!

37. Towards self-mastery

As a human being, you naturally aspire to achieve something. You want to be a contribution to your environment. You want to be of value to people around you. Of course, in the process you want to experience joy, happiness, and fulfillment. However, in order to be effective in giving to others and the environment, you have to be in control of yourself. To change the world around you, for the better, you have to change yourself, along the way, for the better. You are a work in progress.

What is self-mastery in relation to your life? This simply means that you must have balance in, and between, the major areas of your life: finance and career, relationships, health, spirituality, and personal empowerment and recreation. These underlying elements provide the foundation for achieving balance in your life:

- Your passion for living. The activities that give you joy.
- Your commitment to act consistently to pursue your passion.
- The continuous proper daily use of twenty four hours.
- Filling your mind with worthwhile information and wisdom.
- Keeping company with eagles, and not chickens.
- Keeping your positive and negative emotions under control.
- Accept the reality around you, without being anxious to change it immediately.

- Accept people, and situations, for what they are, and you will avoid inner frustration, emotional turmoil, worries, and depression.
- Change yourself, through positive self-mastery, and the world around you will change for the better, reflecting your own changes.

Self-mastery is not about perfectionism, nor do you have to be as evolved as Buddha or Jesus to be self-mastered. If you were sent on a quest to find "the perfect tree," after investigation and discussion you would probably conclude that there is no one perfect tree. It is the same with human beings. Each of us has his/her own unique way! This concept applies in the same way to self-mastery. Your quest is to be the most excellent person that you can be. Optimize your own uniqueness!

38. What are your concerns about your life?

You have been reading these inspirational nuggets in this book. How has the material impacted on you? Answer these questions to get an insight into the impact on your life.

- What topic area so far has been most useful to you?
- What topic area would you most want to pursue in the future?
- What is your greatest challenge at present?
- What is the greatest frustration facing you?
- What is stopping you from getting what you want in life?

Consider these questions carefully, and document the answers..

Perhaps you will see a pattern that you need to address. You also should examine whether you are placing the blame somewhere else, instead of in your own court.

You can raise to great heights, if you continue to follow the systems and processes developed in the reflections in this book. The questions raised above, have within them the seeds of the answers. Keep at it!

39. Clarify what you stand for

What makes you tick? Who are you, and what do you stand for?

It may be useful at this point to clarify what you stand for.

Ask yourself these questions:

- What are my values?
- What do I stand for?
- What are my core beliefs?
- What virtues do I aspire to?
- What will I not stand for?
- What would I sacrifice for, suffer for, and perhaps even die for?

These are extremely important questions to answer, and they can help you to excel in life. From your answers to these questions, select your three top key values, and write them down.

Every choice or decision you make is based on your values, but when you consciously choose, you bring power to your decision. These action exercises will help you to be consistent in your choices.

Action Exercises:

[1] Having clarified your three top core beliefs and your unifying principles, assess your life today, in relation to them, to confirm that you are keeping in integrity with yourself.

[2] If you conclude that you are slipping with respect to holding true to your core values and beliefs, then take one small step to make your life better. Take another small step and keep the momentum going, and I will see you at the top!

40. Every difficulty has within it new opportunities

The universal law is that every condition has both a positive and a negative aspect. These two polarities are necessary for things to be manifested and for distinctions to be possible. An example is that unless there is the contrast of both light and darkness, the concepts will not be understood. Thus, a person born blind from birth will not have the distinction of light.

The law of compensation requires that every negative has a positive. You cannot have the bad without the good. With every loss comes a gain. Every difficulty has within it the seeds of an opportunity. What this means is that you have the possibility to extract from any experience something that can be used for your benefit, and towards achieving your goals.

Seeing in every experience the strands that can link to your success may be the key to push you on to victory where others only see disappointment. Remember that a stumble may prevent a fall.

Day 6 review

You have reflected for the past 5 days on different Inspirational Reflections in this book. You should now indicate what insights you got from your reading. List below at least 2 or 3 insights that you got from the Reflections, or information that was reinforced or confirmed.

_____

_____

_____

_____

Day 7 review

You have reflected for the past 6 days on different Inspirational Reflections. To get the best from the material, list below at least 2 areas or particular situations in your life in which you commit to do better.

_____

_____

_____

_____

41. Give that which you want, and you will receive it

There are five basic things most persons want in life:

• love • money • friendship • health • peace of mind

Your new approach should be to focus on giving rather than on receiving, or desiring. These efforts will produce tangible results, not previously experienced. In fact they express the underlying "Law of Attraction," that operates in all areas of life. The key to the operation of the law of giving is that it must be done unconditionally. Remember the proverbs you heard from childhood?

• It is more blessed to give than to receive
• If you want a friend, be a friend

You must not give with the specific objective of getting back in return. You give because you want to give, not for the person to be obligated to you for giving. In this way you have no expectations from the person you benefited.

If you want peace of mind, let your every thought, word and action towards others be:

• constructive • positive • uplifting • life supporting.

Live your life with graciousness and gratitude.

42. Re-invent yourself

Fear and poverty can diminish you. Security now is in BUILDING YOURSELF and YOUR PERSONAL VALUES. It is in MAKING YOURSELF OVER and rebuilding your habits, character, and thoughts. Yes, you must rebuild and reprogram yourself.

A New Beginning is just a thought away. Life is 10% what happens to "you" and 90% what you do with what happens to "you."

Over time, your level of abundance and prosperity will unfold in direct proportion to your level of personal growth. So, you have to ask yourself this question, "How much is it worth for me to grow?" You love yourself and YOU believe in your own power. You do. So now is the time to show it. Take a bold step.

It's so EASY to be distracted right now. Give yourself the GIFT of focus. Give yourself the GIFT of courage. Give yourself the GIFT of taking ONE step at a time. You don't have to get it right, you just have to get it going. The key to success is a function of your attitude multiplied by your skills. Increase your ability through education. Formal education makes you a living, and combined with self-education makes you a fortune.

Are you ready to increase your self-confidence 1% today? Are you ready to take 1% more action today in your life or business? Are you ready to give 1% more today? Are you ready to say YES to your greatness?

I honor you, appreciate you, and believe in you, especially as you are reading these inspirational reflections. Now, position yourself for the world to celebrate you. Polish your skill set, and empower yourself by reflecting on what needs to be done in your life now, and do it. Have faith in your potential, and live your dreams powerfully!

43. Think and act for success

You have many good thoughts, but that is not good enough. Good thoughts by themselves do not make you a success. A good thought translates to success through effective action. Whether you take action, depends on your own motivation. If you are deeply committed and involved in the desires of your heart, you will take the appropriate action to manifest those thoughts. Wishing is the easy step in the thinking process. When you do not act on your thoughts, you later reflect—I could have. I should have. I ought to have. The fact is that you were a wishful thinker.

Don't be dismayed. Consider the fact that many rich and successful people started with nothing but their ideas and enthusiasm. The path they traveled was strewn with confusion, struggle, challenge, and opportunity. They persisted. With each small success, their path got easier, and with consistency it was turned into a superhighway of success. You can also create your own superhighway of success

Stand up for what you think and believe. Move beyond merely being a thinker, and be a doer. Decide what you want out of life, then be action oriented. Be internally motivated. Fulfill your desires through relevant consistent action. If you want to be a success, you have to move from one action to another action, without losing momentum and enthusiasm.

44. Your actions today determine your life tomorrow

I had dinner with a matured medical practitioner who had traveled the world. He was married twice, had adult children, and was now in somewhat of a challenged financial situation. His conversation was enlightening and intelligent. In the middle of our discussions, he explained that the position he found himself in was his destiny.

I squirmed, and enquired whether he was disclaiming responsibility for what had happened to him. I posited that if our destiny was pre-determined in the sense that some superior being divined it, then there is no need for an individual to make effort. No matter what he does he is destined to a particular condition. This would certainly not be the wish of a Divine Creator. In fact, this would deny the concept of individual choice on a moment-to-moment basis. After discussion, the Doctor agreed that a person's own individual action is crucial to that person's future.

I thought about this some more, and came to the conclusion that this is something you should reflect on, as very subtly a skewed concept of destiny could lead you, quite unintentionally, to give up taking the steps and making the efforts that are needed to make your dreams come true.

Your choice is your power. Ensure that you continue to make choices and take massive action consistent with what is necessary to convert your dreams to reality. You have to move your dreams from your head to paper, or digital form. This is the first step to move your dreams along to fruition. If you do not release them from your head and tongue, they will remain in your head and be just dreams-never to be realized. Take wise action on your dreams today. You can do it!

45. There is opportunity and possibility in every calamity

Every situation has the seeds of opportunity, as well as the seeds of disappointment. You therefore have the choice of letting calamity get you down, or turning the searchlight on calamity to discover the opportunity that has opened up for you.

You can use your creative insight to see the new vistas that are now available through what appears to be a calamity. Being an optimist does not mean that you have to be unrealistic. You can be a person who sees the reality of new possibilities from distraught situations. You will ordinarily recognize when things are in your favor and react positively.

At one extreme, you can be so negative, that rather than see an opportunity that presents itself, you see the risks and the dangers attached to moving to exploit the opportunity. However, you must also be aware that when things seem to be against you, there is always a silver lining in the cloud. Seek out that silver lining.

Day 6 review

You have reflected for the past 5 days on different Inspirational Reflections in this book. You should now indicate what insights you got from your reading. List below at least 2 or 3 insights that you got from the Reflections, or information that was reinforced or confirmed.

_____

_____

_____

_____

Day 7 review

You have reflected for the past 6 days on different Inspirational Reflections. To get the best from the material, list below at least 2 areas or particular situations in your life in which you commit to do better.

_____

_____

_____

_____

Day 7 review

You have reflected for the past 6 days. For different inspirational Reflexions. To get the best from the material, list below at least 2 areas or particular situations in your life in which you currently struggle.

CHAPTER 2: RISE TO THE CHALLENGE

46. Are you blessed?

You saw daylight today. You are alive, not yet gone to the Great Beyond. Thus, there is tremendous possibility for your life. You have received untold blessings during the past 12 months, although you may not be fully conscious of them. You have your sight, hearing, ability to walk, housing accommodation, and the list goes on and on.

Pause and acknowledge your many blessings. Display an attitude of gratitude, and it will open new doors of success. The next 12 months is a period to impact your life as you never did before. The key to your future is not to make new resolutions, since over the years your many resolutions have not been rigorously followed. You have a backlog of unfinished business—unfinished resolutions.

As you look ahead, consider what important resolutions of the past you did not pursue assiduously. Re-commit to them, if they are still relevant to you, and develop plans and projects to deliver them during the next 12 months.

You can do it because you have seen the wisdom of their benefits. Grasp the opportunities to impact your life in the way that you believe will bring out your brilliance, and display your potential and talents. This is your opportunity for ultimate success. Go for it!

47. Be Respectful to be successful

Being respectful is an important factor in achieving the success you want in life. The wisdom of the ages dictates this. When you treat people as if they are exuding their potential, you will help them become what they are capable of becoming.

Respectful, according to Webster's dictionary, means: to feel or show honor or esteem for; hold in high regard; to consider or treat with deference or dutiful regard. We recommend that you put the following words to action:

R - respectful, responsible, reassure
E - educate, encourage, evolve
S - sincere, sympathetic, support
P - praise, practice, patience
E - encouragement, enjoyment, enthusiasm
C - communicate, cuddle, compliment
T - truth, trust, tenderness
F - faithfulness, fulfillment, fun
U - understand, unite, uplift
L - listen, learn, love, laugh

Select three of the words above that you believe you could improve in your life, and work assiduously with them for the next three months. You will be surprised at the positive changes in your life.

At one time, the three words that I worked on were compliment, tenderness, and learn. I needed to encourage and compliment persons around me more than I did then. My harsh experiences in life had made me uncompromisingly harsh at times: I needed to develop more tenderness and compassion. Learners are leaders, and you are on the learning curve until you die. I must not let past events close my mind to new things, and new opportunities. Select your own three words, and enjoy the personal growth you experience by acting on them.

48. All things are possible

When you believe you can accomplish something, you are really visioning that it is possible. When you think that something is not possible, you have an absence of positive belief about that thing. The basis of belief is your view that there is a real possibility that what you believe you can do, can be accomplished.

You can kill or weaken your belief by introducing doubt. However, your mind does not know whether what you believe is in fact the truth. The mind transmits that belief through your emotional, psychological, mental, bodily and spiritual systems. There is the popular adage, that faith or belief can move mountains.

The Holy Scriptures confirm that it will be done unto you as you believe. The key to optimizing your belief system then, is to become aware that all things are possible. When you remove the limitations of your present knowledge, and stand in the gap fielding all possibilities, you can achieve your full, and best potential.

49. Challenging success techniques

Success can be defined in many ways. To make it simple, let us say that success is achieving what you set out to be and do. Five key elements to pursue to guarantee your success are;

- Be clear on what you want, and be passionate about it.
- Visualize, and affirm your intentions.
- Establish your goals and plans.
- Take massive consistent relevant action
- Celebrate and enjoy your successes

Challenges to overcome in pursuit of your success are:

- Ensure that you really want it, and it is not the dream of someone else. It must be your desire, and you must really be keen, and upbeat about it.
- You have to see it in your mind's eye before you can believe it. Also, be careful that your affirmation is not so unreal that it amounts to your telling yourself a lie.
- Your goals must stretch you, so they are not easily accomplished. But they must not be so outrageous that you set yourself up to fail.
- Action must be timely, and unreservedly promote attainment of your goals.
- You need to celebrate milestones of success on your journey, as this fuels your success momentum.

You have the ability and potential to get what you want in life, and to become the person you want to be. Resolve today to do something different in keeping with the life you want to experience. Challenge yourself to conquer new frontiers you imagined. You can do it!

50. Relentless focus helps you achieve your goals

What you put your attention on grows stronger in your life. Energy focused is powerful. The rays of the sun have power but when they are channeled through a magnifying glass, the focus of the rays become so powerful that what is in its path is burned.

A similar focus and singleness of purpose are required for success in life, no matter what aspect of life is being pursued. One Sage commented that success in life depends on regularity of action; regularity produces singularity, and singularity produces "Samadhi" or happiness, which in turn can be raised to the level of fulfillment. If you apply yourself wholly and fully to one thing at a time you have a good chance of success. If you get involved with too many things at the same time, you will spread yourself so thin that no area will be well covered.

Concentration is the magic key to success. Focus your effort on a single point and you will achieve the greatest results.

Day 6 review

You have reflected for the past 5 days on different Inspirational Reflections in this book. You should now indicate what insights you got from your reading. List below at least 2 or 3 insights that you got from the Reflections, or information that was reinforced or confirmed.

_____

_____

_____

_____

Day 7 review

You have reflected for the past 6 days on different Inspirational Reflections. To get the best from the material, list below at least 2 areas or particular situations in your life in which you commit to do better.

_____

_____

_____

_____

51. Your Champion's Creed

You live your life based on a series of beliefs. Sometimes you are conscious of the values you are pursuing, but many times you act automatically on a daily basis, as matters confront you.

It is a useful exercise to record what are the major values or beliefs that govern your life. This is oft times referred to as a Creed, and since you aspire to be a Champion, document what is Your Champion's Creed.

Consider each line, and if you have any doubt, work on strengthening that particular line that you are not embracing 100%. This will help you to progress with your dreams.

To give an example of a Champion's Creed, this is what I explained as my Creed in a book I co-authored with Stephen Covey et al, entitled, *Discover Your Inner Strength*. My Creed stated therein simply is:

> I see the brighter side of situations
> I speak the positive side of things
> I communicate with energy
> I listen attentively
> I encourage others
> I keep continuously acclaiming the good in others
> I forgive myself for any limitations
> I forgive others who hurt me
> I am kind to all

I seek to bring out the best in myself

I help others to rise to their best potential

I acknowledge that there is a Supreme Creative Force, and that

I am a spark of it, and that is my life.

Develop your own Champion's Creed, and continue to live a life of learning, growing, and being fulfilled.

52. Change your thoughts to change your life

Every action that you take, has its origin as a thought. The sum of all the actions you take, produce the person that you are. Change the thoughts that govern your actions, and you will change your life.

To impact your life, go to the root cause. Examine your thinking which produces your personal success or failure. Life is full of challenges. Life is full of obstacles. Life is full of opportunities. It is therefore certain that your life will be a rough road. So what? That is the name of the game of life.

You have been designed with a mind that has great and wonderful power. Use it wisely to give you confidence instead of timidity, clarity instead of confusion, balance instead of restlessness, and peace of mind rather than heartache.

The first step in the formula to help you change your thoughts to become a better person is to practice the 3 C's. Do not Complain ! Do not Criticize ! Do not Condemn! Try it for just one hour every day for 30 consecutive days, and you will become a new and better person.

53. Core values facilitate your success

Your personal success depends on exercising values of discipline, service, honor, and their derivatives. Discipline can be defined as doing what needs to be done, when it needs to be done although you do not feel like doing it. Do not let your feelings govern your actions. Feelings, in this context, means the emotional response to a situation that is triggered by the sloppy and negative vibrations that fill your immediate environment. It does not mean your intuition.

Service, which is one of the gateways to enlightenment, must be distinguished from servitude under slavery. The command to love your neighbor as yourself has within it the seeds of service. Whatever your skills, talents, gifts and attributes, you too can be a contribution of service to others, in some way, and thus carve your own success and greatness.

One of the Commandments handed down to Moses states, "Honor thy father and thy mother that thy days may be long upon the land which the Lord thy God giveth thee." This suggests that 'honor' is a powerful concept at the root of success. Honor is high respect and public regard; adhering to what is right, or to what is an accepted standard of conduct; nobleness of mind.

Exercise personal discipline, service and honor vigorously, and you will produce amazing results of success.

54. Reflecting on your motives

You are motivated by what induces you to act, or to choose. When you know and understand the principles that motivate, you can use them to achieve what you want out of life. You follow through with action on your motivation when you desire something, value it, and truly believe that it is attainable.

There are ten basic motives for action and any one of them or a combination is at the base of every thought, or voluntary and involuntary action.

Of these motives, five are for the **DESIRE** of:

- self-preservation
- recognition and self-expression
- freedom of body and mind
- material gain
- life after death.

The other five motives are **EMOTIONS** of:

- love
- hate
- fear
- sex
- anger.

The negative emotions of fear, hate and anger must be kept in balance to ensure your success. There are special times when they may properly apply. For example, fear God, hate doing evil and be angry with injustice. Govern your desires and emotions by constantly observing the virtues of temperance, sincerity, justice, moderation and humility. Persist with the enquiry into your deeper purpose of life.

55. Prepare to accomplish your desires

Luck has been defined as preparation meeting opportunity. Confidence has been defined as knowing that you know. When you combine these two definitions of luck and confidence, you have the beginnings of being able to be ready for any eventuality.

You first have to determine what you want out of life and then you can prepare to accomplish it. Preparation is essential. The boy scouts clarion call, "be prepared," expresses the point succinctly. While you may have natural skills and ability, they will be enhanced by due preparation.

When you are prepared for whatever it is you wish to accomplish in life, the opportunity usually presents itself. In any event, it is better that you are prepared, and the opportunity does not come, than you are not prepared and the opportunity comes. It is interesting, that usually when you are prepared for a particular occurrence, somehow, the opportunity seems to present itself. When you are prepared you will know that you know, and you can then go forth in confidence.

Day 6 review

You have reflected for the past 5 days on different Inspirational Reflections in this book. You should now indicate what insights you got from your reading. List below at least 2 or 3 insights that you got from the Reflections, or information that was reinforced or confirmed.

_____

_____

_____

_____

Day 7 review

You have reflected for the past 6 days on different Inspirational Reflections. To get the best from the material, list below at least 2 areas or particular situations in your life in which you commit to do better.

_____

_____

_____

56. Step into your greatness

Have you been looking forward to step into your greatness? You do not have to get anyone's permission for your brilliance to shine. You can best excel, if you take inspired action. When you have desires, and set goals, if they do not materialize as you expect, this is not failure. A missed goal is merely deferred success, if you continue to take relevant committed action consistent with that goal.

Follow these guidelines, and you will certainly manifest your greatness:

- Determine the reasons for what you want in life. The more powerful the reasons, the easier it is to overcome distractions, obstacles, and challenges.
- Every week take at least one relevant action step (not thinking or speaking, but taking action) towards your heart's desire. Be consistent, committed, and persistent.
- Celebrate whatever small successes you achieve on your journey. Reward sweetens your efforts. Enjoy your journey, and your greatness.

57. Celebrate your achievements

When you realize your dreams, or any significant goal, you must find a way to mark the occasion through an appropriate celebration. Why is this? Well, all persons, either consciously or unconsciously, set goals. All persons achieve at least 50% of their goals. But only a few persons enjoy their achievements. Too often you just keep going, without reflecting on how well you have done.

My wife and I enjoyed a cruise on the Caribbean Princess sailing from New York to Halifax and other Canadian seaboard ports. This was my reward for completing my autobiography. It was a refreshing experience celebrating one of my dreams of submitting my autobiography for publication. My three previously published books, and the other that I co-authored at that time, did not give me the same excitement and satisfaction as completion of my autobiography, and I just had to celebrate this.

Why am I sharing this with you? It is to sensitize you to look for opportunities to celebrate your own success. The thrill of the celebration will inspire you to go after your dreams more powerfully. The celebration does not necessarily have to be a cruise. Also, the achievement need not be momentous, although it should be of significance to what you want in life. The celebration can range from an ice ream sundae, to a special dinner, to purchase of jewelry or clothing, or anything that will lift your spirits. The key is the conscious awareness that it is a celebration.

So there you have it. I am sure that you have been achieving goals and sub-goals. This is an opportunity to review what is happening in your life. Go celebrate. Celebrate! Celebrate! Celebrate!

58. People problems

Any problem you have in life can be linked back to some relationship problem with another person. People are at the centre of any problem. Even financial problems are people related. To earn or get more money is almost always related to interaction with other people. The nature and quality of interacting with other people is the challenge of life.

We are all so different, that it puts a strain on our relationships. You can resolve that differences, disputes and disappointments will not deter you from fulfilling your dreams, and being the best that you can be. Just look for the lesson in any encounter, don't repeat what is not life supporting, and learn from the experience.

Work towards mastering your personal encounters. This requires you to be people sensitive. You need first to understand the other person, rather than insisting on the person first understanding you. This approach will ensure that the rough diamond that you are will be polished into a brilliant gem that shines in personal encounters.

59. Personal vision and action revolution

If you want to be a new you, now is the time to make the decision. Others want you to be what they believe is right for you. You can start a personal revolution of YOUR vision and action.

Decide to rise above the criticism, cynicism, fear, and other people's opinions that surround you. Arise, and determine what you stand for, and what you want out of life. This is the beginning of your Personal Vision, and Action Revolution.

If you are committed to the new you, the Revolution begins Now—as you read this! You can live life to its fullest expression for you by considering:

- How can I maintain my values in times of self-doubt, insecurity, and loneliness?
- How can I keep the mindset that I can everyday work towards attainment of my goals, despite how I may be tempted to feel?
- How can I keep my vision, when no one around me sees, or supports it?

Reviewing these questions will help you to make a difference, no matter the size of that difference. This is what will give you and your family a better future. Understand that you have the ability to develop a sense of knowing that nothing, or no one, can stop you from achieving your personal vision and action revolution. Be persistent, committed, and unstoppable!

60. Your uniqueness and individuality

In each person there is the Higher Self and the lower self. These two forces represent the positive and the negative aspects of life. You are spirit, body and soul. These three elements combine to express your individuality. The spirit is eternal and represents the spark of Divinity. The soul consists of the mind, the intellect and all the other senses, and these exist at the gross level.

The spirit exists at the subtle level and there is the continuous clash between the gross and the subtle levels. Part of the problem is that the mind and intellect only know in part and do not have all pervading knowledge of the Higher Self, that part of you which is a hologram of the Supreme Being.

The imperfect nature of the lower self tends to resist the directions of the Higher Self. One way of reducing the conflict between the two warring forces is by listening more intently to the whisperings you hear from your intuitive voice. Learn to be still and enter the silence, in order to access the streaming from your Higher Self.

Day 6 review

You have reflected for the past 5 days on different Inspirational Reflections in this book. You should now indicate what insights you got from your reading. List below at least 2 or 3 insights that you got from the Reflections, or information that was reinforced or confirmed.

_____

_____

_____

_____

Day 7 review

You have reflected for the past 6 days on different Inspirational Reflections. To get the best from the material, list below at least 2 areas or particular situations in your life in which you commit to do better.

_____

_____

_____

_____

Choose prosperity and conquer poverty

61.The Power of Fear

Fear is the view you have that an event in the future will not be what you want it to be. In a sense, it is the opposite of your having faith that the future event will occur in the manner that you want.

Fear is a two-edged sword. It can stop you from growing into whom you can be. However, it can also avoid you from courting danger. For example, a motor-car may be speeding when, as a pedestrian, you are about to cross the road. Fear of the car hitting you may delay your crossing the road, but this is a life giving fear.

You may also consider that it is not fear that stopped you from crossing the road, but reason. Sometimes there is a thin dividing line between reason and fear. Remember that reason has limits, since you never have all the relevant information. Faith has no limits if you believe that it is possible.

Fear is created in your own mind so you have the power to control it. When you continue in action despite fear, you eventually overcome the fear. Move from fear of the future, to faith in the future.

Fear is an essential part of life. Some fears help you, but most fears pester you. Identify what fears help you, harness and keep them under control.

Recognize the fears that harm you, work on them, and eventually overcome them. Although effective removal of harmful fears takes time, you can do it.

62. Re-program your thinking

The biggest setback for success in your life is the information with which you saturate your mind. When you were a child growing up much garbage was dumped in your mind without your knowing it consciously.

You were streamed with negative information, The effect of this, not deliberately intended by your loved ones, was to produce negativity in your life such as:

- Lack of confidence
- Self-sabotage
- Weakness
- Indecisiveness
- Negative mental attitude
- Negative self-talk, and much more negativity.

You now have the power to break those negative bonds. Examine your recurring thoughts, your self-image, your beliefs about money, and your relationships with the people with whom you spend most time.

There are many approaches that can be used when you are examining your life to propel you to the next higher rung of success. However, one model is to consider the 7 C's.

The first four are affirmative and deal mainly with your personal interactions. The other three deal primarily with your inner responses to events. They are:

- Commitment
- Communication
- Courtesy
- Compassion
- Complain (do not, especially about yourself)
- Criticize (do not, especially about yourself)
- Condemn (do not, especially about yourself)

Your mind is more powerful than the most sophisticated computer on the planet. Use the power of your mind to create the successful and happy life that you want. You can do it! Start with one small step at a time, and keep the momentum going.

63. What is your dream?

Your life unfolds as a flower. As you grow out of babyhood and become aware of yourself and others, you begin to design your life. You develop desires and convert them into dreams. At all points in your life you have dreams. But are they your dreams?

Quite often your dreams are those of your parents, your teachers, your spouse or your friends. If the dream is not your own, your actions and plans are being set by someone else. When your dreams are not your own, you still have the responsibility to do all that you can to ensure that your life evolves in relation to those dreams.

If you are not clear about what you want, how you propose to get it, the cost of getting it, and the benefits you will receive from achieving it, you will not be living your full life.

Take responsibility for your life and live it to the best of your ability. What are you passionate about these days? What is the spark that drives you to action, as you face challenges every day? Confront yourself now, and revisit your compelling dream. If you cannot find what it is that makes your life worth living, you have an opportunity today to reflect, and shoot for your star. Everyone has a special destiny to fulfill. Honor your special destiny. Use your talents to live fully with ease, comfort, a healthy state, and a positive attitude.

64. Seize the moment

You have to accept the reality of what is happening to you, and around you. What happens within, forms your attitude. Your attitude may be empowering, or it may be one of negativity, self-pity, complaining, criticizing, or condemning.

Ask 3 crucial questions in any given situation, if you wish to maintain an empowering attitude:

- What is great about this situation? There is always something of value that you can point to in any situation. Search for it!
- What can I learn from this encounter? When learning stops, the mind deteriorates. The principle—use it or lose it—also applies to your brain. Learn a lesson from every experience.
- What needs to change to make the situation what I would like it to be? This enquiry will engender your being open, curious, innovative, and productive.

It is not the circumstances of your life that determine your success:

it is the manner in which you respond to those circumstances. You can take control of your life. Seize the moment!

65. A blend of habit and reasoning balance your life

Can you remember which shoe you put on first this morning? Was it on your left foot or your right foot? The answer is illustrative. Either you cannot remember, or you put on the same side that you have habitually put on first. Habit is so strong in your life that you act automatically in many areas, without first thinking. That is the reason why sometimes after you have left home you wonder whether you turned off the stove or locked the door.

However, make no mistake, without habits life would be tiresome. Since habit is so powerful, you need to ensure that you are not operating on automatic habit for all of the 24 hours in the day. Such reflection is important as the habit that was established in the first place might not have been well thought out.

Moreover, changed circumstances and new knowledge might make the old habit inappropriate. Old habits are difficult to replace, so make sure that your habits are good habits, and that they can withstand the scrutiny of your reasoning.

Day 6 review

You have reflected for the past 5 days on different Inspirational Reflections in this book. You should now indicate what insights you got from your reading. List below at least 2 or 3 insights that you got from the Reflections, or information that was reinforced or confirmed.

_____

_____

_____

_____

Day 7 review

You have reflected for the past 6 days on different Inspirational Reflections. To get the best from the material, list below at least 2 areas or particular situations in your life in which you commit to do better.

_____

_____

_____

_____

66. Take action when opportunity knocks

My friend, Ray, of 36 years association has many fine qualities, but his success is fuelled by his laser like focus, and alacrity of action. The interesting aspect of Ray's life is that he stopped his formal education at primary school level. He worked up his way from the bottom of the corporate ladder through self-improvement programs, and his grit and determination helped him to become:

- In charge of the Caribbean Region of one of the largest insurance companies in the world
- Promoter and founder of a life insurance company in Trinidad and Tobago
- Creator, owner and master therapist of one of the top Pain Relief Institutes in the Caribbean

You can be successful also, if you have passion, determination, and you take a stand about eliminating procrastination. There are many dreams you have had, but you did not follow up with dedicated action. There was always some fear that stopped you from taking action. You preferred to remain in your comfort zone. Success (whatever that means to you) follows action.

Resolve today to take one action that you have been postponing, which if you did take could make a big positive difference in your life.

Get ahead with your life through taking action, being focused, and not delaying. If you want to get ahead, get started. The secret of getting started is to reduce complex and large issues into small manageable tasks, and then starting on the first one

Sometimes in your life an opportunity knocks. When this happens you can accept it, make the most of it, or simply let it pass you by. There are "Infinite Possibilities" available to you. There may have been several during the past two years. Consider what opportunity may be knocking on your door of life, and go forward bravely into action. You owe it to yourself and to your family.

67. What will you achieve in the next five years?

Before you answer the question, I need to share with you a comment sent to me by a Trinidadian client I coach who resides in the USA. He e-mailed me in relation to the political campaign of then President Elect Obama:

> "WINNING THE WHITE HOUSE by Barack Obama was poetry in motion.
>
> We witnessed the PURPOSE identified...PASSION demonstrated...
>
> PROCESS actioned...the PRIZE achieved.
>
> We saw the winner take advantage of the technological revolution ...use teaming as the strategic imperative... and project with sincerity, collaboration as his leadership

style. The sale was closed….."THE GREATEST SALE OF THE CENTURY."

Now back to the question. Posed at the start of this Reflection. The person you will become in the next 5 years is a function of two things. First, what goes in your mind: the books you read, the things you listen to, and what you view. Your mind provides your leverage for success. Second, the company you keep. The people with whom you associate, limit or expand personal growth and success. A mediocre environment can halt your ambition. It can almost dry it up. Ambition was created to be aroused.

One of the greatest ways to arouse your ambition is spending time in pro-growth environments and around people that are always moving forward. Environment has a great deal to do with your ambition and achievement. Keep close to people who inspire and encourage you, who communicate enthusiasm by their example If you surround yourself with discordant conditions, and associate with toxic people it will have a negative effect on your progress.

There's a sleeping giant that lives within you. Awaken it! Empower yourself. Act now, by doing what you already know needs to be done, for access to the greatness of your brilliance!

68. Thanksgiving

The United States of America celebrates ever year its holiday of Thanksgiving. What really does "Thanksgiving" mean to you? Put simply, it is a sense of gratitude to reflect on the goodness in your life, and honor that bounty. Quite often you focus on what's missing in your life, and pay scant attention to what you have.

I was speaking to a client who had both eyes operated on, and for 24 hours thereafter her eyes were blindfolded and she could not see. When the bandages were removed she was ecstatic. She said, "Philip, I really appreciated my sight in those darkened 24 hours. I did not know where I was. I was completely disoriented moving about the house, although my daughter was guiding me. I felt lost."

Another client told me how he called a friend, who since his wife died was perpetually depressed. My client started to tell his friend over the telephone how he should be thankful for his blessings, and his friend slammed the telephone in his ear. Half an hour later the friend telephoned, apologized for his behavior, and thanked his friend for his concern. The depressed friend then said, "I reflected, and appreciated my children are around me, I am not destitute, and I have my sight, hearing and use of my legs. I am shifting to an attitude of gratitude. I am thankful."

You do not have to go through an eye operation or death of a spouse to recognize that there are many blessings for which you can be thankful. Give thanks! Reflect on all the goodness that is in your life, and celebrate.

Every day I give thanks that I have good health for my age, that I am loved by my family and close friends, and I am mentally stable. When you appreciate what you have, and give thanks, you open the windows of heaven for more blessings to be showered on you. Light a candle of thanksgiving rather than murmur about what's missing in your life. Celebrate life, and all that it has bestowed on you.

69. Time is a precious gift that allows your fulfillment

Time is a precious gift that allows your fulfillment. Between your birth and death there is a definitive time period. Time, your most precious gift, is made up of the past, present, and future. Your concept of these time horizons will greatly influence your success.

Remember that the past does not equal the future. The past is hindsight, and the future is mind sight—vision and possibility. The present is reality. It is now that matters, as from it you fashion your future. The past can reveal important lessons. However, dwelling on, or living in, the past can be likened to driving a car, while steadfastly looking in the rear view mirror. You will surely crash. The past has important lessons for you, learn them, but do not live in the past.

Time is a great healer, and in the fullness of time all things are possible. To get the best out of time, do not be bound by the past, nor limited by the present, nor live merely wishing about the future.

Resolve to determine your future and destiny by possibility thinking, and creative action. Your future vision determines how you address your present. Learn from the lessons of the past, so you do not repeat the same errors, and thus make better current choices. You have the power to be what you want to be. Arise, act, and achieve.

70. Become part of the learning revolution

I remember that at the end of my first year at University in the United Kingdom, I began to walk like a lion—powerful, proud, strong and self-confident. I had read more books, periodicals and other material in that first year than the average person reads in a lifetime.

By the time of my graduation I was humbled. I changed my walk from that of a lion to that of a lamb. I became conscious of how ignorant I was. It was true that my knowledge put me in the top 10% of the knowledgeable people of the country. However, I became conscious while reading for the degree that I knew more and more of less and less. This made me reflect on the adage, " He who knows not, and knows that he knows not is a wise man, cultivate him."

Be conscious of the great strides that are taking place in knowledge daily. Resolve to close your knowledge gap by gathering information dally in a consistent, structured manner. The world is moving at a rapid pace of change. You need to match those changes by increasing your knowledge base. Read, or listen to at least one book every 2 months.

Day 6 review

You have reflected for the past 5 days on different Inspirational Reflections in this book. You should now indicate what insights you got from your reading. List below at least 2 or 3 insights that you got from the Reflections, or information that was reinforced or confirmed.

_____

_____

_____

_____

Day 7 review

You have reflected for the past 6 days on different Inspirational Reflections. To get the best from the material, list below at least 2 areas or particular situations in your life in which you commit to do better.

_____

_____

_____

_____

71. Use your talents wisely

You have many talents. Focus on one of them, and make a difference to the people around you. You are multitalented, so you are tempted to consider doing many things, and in the process you do little of significance. Be laser like in your focus, and use the unique talents that you have.

There are four approaches you can take:

- Choose something that you get joy from doing, whether you are paid for it or not. A test for its relevance to you is that you must be passionate about the activity.
- Consider who can benefit from the use of the talents that produce joy for you. The activity must also produce "light" in the lives of others.
- Commit to the relentless pursuit of bringing joy, or relief to others while you get joy from the activities. You cannot spray perfume on another, without getting some of it on yourself.
- Start where you are now, with what you have. Do not wait for conditions to be right, as they will never be. Start with one small step. Take another small step, and another. Keep the momentum going, and soon you will see positive results in your life.

Do something different during the next few days. You owe it to yourself.

72. Wealth and poverty can be both blessings

Wealth, accumulation of worldly goods and money, is not a bad thing, if you have obtained it honestly. If you then use it wisely, including giving to charity, wealth is a blessing.

How you get wealth, and how you use it, determine whether it is a blessing or curse. Poverty, or the absence of your being able to have minimum of food, clothes and shelter, is not necessarily a curse. At first glance, it may be considered a curse. However, the iron law of survival can draw out the best within you to convert your poverty into an overwhelming drive for financial freedom. Moreover, poverty quite often is the trigger to get you to put your attention on spiritual matters.

Thus, poverty can drive you to new heights of spiritual growth and financial independence. God's very nature is abundance and not scarcity, so if you are made in His image and likeness you can claim your inheritance of abundant prosperity. It starts in your mind. Think abundance, think prosperity, and use your God given talents wisely.

73. What "word" leads to growth in your success?

Too often you say "no" to an opportunity, so consider the possibilities before you reject your future. Greatness Starts By Saying YES to An Opportunity.

Look around you right now. There's an opportunity for you to do something great. There's an opportunity to get around more action oriented individuals. There's an opportunity to bring a great coach in your life.

Can you imagine yourself as being great. Close your eyes and see yourself being a success. It might be tough, but do it. Unfold into your best self. Love yourself. Be your best self. Get off your lethargy and get into activity.

I urge you dear reader to select wisely from one of my books,

"Infinite Possibilities," and you will generate "Infinite Success." It is very easy to say "no" to an opportunity, as then you do not have to extend yourself. When you say "yes" to an opportunity, it very often means moving out of your comfort zone, and doing things that require special effort.

Be confident that you can say "yes" to an opportunity, and rise to the challenge of performance. You have great potential. You can accomplish anything you put your attention on.

74. Commit your energy to what you truly believe

Life's patterns sometimes create difficulties in your finances, relationships, career, health and spirituality. Do not be dismayed. Do not be discouraged. Reflect on where you are now, and with what you have been blessed. Think about what you have, and not about what's missing. If you have survived to date, whatever you desire can be yours with committed relevant action.

Nature does not provide a clear path in the forest. You have to clear a path to travel. Similarly, life does not provide a smooth passage for you to travel. Circumstances will not always be what are necessary for you to accomplish your goals, or to achieve your desires. What is clear is that you have the power within you to accomplish anything you really want badly enough. Dare to believe in yourself. Dare to act. Dare to speak. Dare to sacrifice your time, money, energy and relationships for what you truly believe you want, and the prize will be yours.

Be courageous, and know that your mind and power are sufficient to climb your highest mountain. Dedicate yourself to success, and live up to your brilliance.

75. Your golden victory is to conquer yourself

A friend of mine who plays golf regularly said that one of his traits is to try to control and direct everyone and everything around him. On reflection, he saw the difficulty of this fetish to control, as he was not even able to control a small golf ball. At each hole on the golf course, he could not sink the ball in the number of strokes he desired.

Then there is the story of the man who was reflecting on his dying bed. As a young man in his 20's he tried to integrate the Caribbean People and he failed. In his 30's he tried to change the people of Trinidad and Tobago to be more National conscious, and he failed. In his 50's he tried to change his immediate community; he failed. In his 60's he tried to change his family to become well knitted and thereby impact other families. He failed.

Now in his 70's, on his dying bed he understood that the only thing he really had control over was himself. He could conquer his fears, foibles and failures. If he conquered himself, he would be the model that would lead others to conquer themselves. The golden victory is thus to conquer your own self. Reflect, and act to conquer yourself. That is, do all in your power to release the uniqueness that you have to offer the world.

Day 6 review

You have reflected for the past 5 days on different Inspirational Reflections in this book. You should now indicate what insights you got from your reading. List below at least 2 or 3 insights that you got from the Reflections, or information that was reinforced or confirmed.

_____

_____

_____

_____

Day 7 review

You have reflected for the past 6 days on different Inspirational Reflections. To get the best from the material, list below at least 2 areas or particular situations in your life in which you commit to do better.

_____

_____

_____

_____

76. Reaching beyond your frustration

Every day you reflect on where you are, and you are just not getting the results you want. Stop thinking that the grass is greener, elsewhere. Start thinking of your own grass—your greatest self. Start to believe in yourself, and that you have the brilliance to make your dreams come true.

The best thing in life is to raise yourself to your highest power, to call out the hidden beauties of your potential, and to make yourself attractive and helpful instead of obnoxious or unsympathetic.

Making money is critical, but what accompanies that is making the most of yourself. The biggest reason people fail is through BROKEN FOCUS. (Read that sentence again) A scattered focus leads to a scattered mind, producing scattered results. Get organized and get focused NOW. Decide on a priority activity, and build on it.

Your greatest self lives within you. To get at an ounce of gold you need to dig through tons of dirt. Through programming, friends, and the environment you have picked up "dirt" over the years. Get rid of that "dirt," and create a focused, orderly environment that will lift you onwards to victory. Victory! It's yours for the taking. Dream big dreams again, and this time take big actions, and persistent relevant actions. Go for it! You can do it!

77. Your invisible and invisible life

Thinking, emotions, spirituality, and the physical world govern your life. Quite often you focus on the visible or physical side of life. This is understandable as your results are evident in the material world.

However, the invisible world and the physical world are not only interdependent, but the invisible worlds of thinking, emotions, and spirituality determine your results in the physical world. Thus, if you want to do better or different in the physical world, the answer is to change how you are behaving in the invisible worlds. You have to change your thinking, emotions, and spirituality.

Put simply, thinking creates desires that in turn create emotions, actions, and an impact on the results in the physical world. Spirituality is evidenced in the manner in which you treat individuals. Being kind to those you can see is a hallmark of spirituality.

But where does your thinking come from? It comes from your programming as a child, and as you grow, from the imprint of what you see, do, hear, read, and the people with whom you associate.

Therefore, you have the possibility as an adult to change your programming, and thereby change both your visible and invisible worlds. Commit to an improved YOU through changing the elements in your invisible world. This will enhance your journey to achieve the life you want. You can do it!

78. From Achiever to Champion Achiever

You have achieved much in your life. However, do you want to be a Champion Achiever? If you want to be a Champion, you need to raise your performance in all critical areas of your life.

Be a champion achiever in your finances and career, relationships, health and diet, spiritual journey, and personal development. To do this you require three elements:

- Clarity of your intention
- Generate passion in carrying out your intention
- Produce consistent unstoppable relevant action

You must be clear about what you want. Your intention must also be precise, and simply expressed to give you power to accomplish it. Generating passion as you pursue your intention is crucial to success. Passion will give you the energy to overcome distractions and hurdles that present themselves.

Action is the element that brings together your intention, and the expected results of your intention. Your action must be structured, and consistent. If you are not consistent, you are non-existent. Consider the consistency of the sun that permits times of daily tides to be known far in advance, and phases of the moon to be correctly predicted.

Moreover, consider the consistency of the action of your heart pumping blood to your whole body, and then resting. This consistency permits the doctor to assess your condition through your resultant heartbeat.

Passion is your emotional response that gives you the fuel of priority over matters that are not really aligned to your key desires. Through new action strive to be a Champion Achiever.

79. Act today for success

Procrastination, or continuously delaying your decision, is a sure way to deny yourself from achieving your heart's desires. Sometimes the mere passage of time does solve problems.

However, more often than not, you have to act in the moment to get the best out of the circumstances, as well as of yourself. The discipline of decision making is to do what needs to be done in the moment, despite your wanting to postpone doing it.

If you have developed a habit of delaying or postponing your decision making, then ask yourself these questions whenever you go into your ritual of postponing:

- Why delay?
- Why not now?
- Why not me?

It is better to act and be wrong, than delay and regret. While your decisions will be wrong some of the time, you will certainly be right sufficiently often to have a positive outcome of your life. Act with urgency, but not recklessly, and your successful growth will be assured.

80. Are you spending your time wisely?

You can either spend your time badly, or invest it wisely. If you spend money, you can work to get more. However, if you spend your time badly, your opportunity is gone forever. You cannot reclaim the lost minute, hour, or day that you have spent. When you spend your time wisely, it is an investment that gives you a return.

You spend your time wisely when you are doing things that will deliver your dreams, and desires. One way to measure the use of your time is to follow these four steps:

- Establish what income you will have to generate on a yearly basis to deliver your goals. (not what you are making at the moment, unless it is sufficient to finance your million dollar desires.)
- Using the yearly income you determined above, work out the hourly rate you will have to receive to meet that annual income. An easy method is to divide the amount by 50, representing 50 working weeks, and then by 40 representing a 40 hour week. For example, if your income yearly target is $100,000, then your hourly rate is $100,000 divided 50, and then by 40 which gives your hourly rate as $50.
- Whenever you are involved in an activity, consider whether it is one that is equivalent to your hourly prospective rate. If it is not, re-assess whether you should be involved in that activity.
- If it is not, consider doing something more worthwhile, and in accord with what you want to achieve. Examples of time wasters are: long personal telephone calls, errands, long lunches, reading

every word in the newspapers or the same stories in different newspapers or several other time stealers.

Success thinkers value their time. They know what they are worth, and are continuously cautious about how they utilize this precious asset of time. Ask yourself the question. Is this activity going to give me a return on my time equal to, or greater than, my hourly worth? A thought you can ponder!

Day 6 review

You have reflected for the past 5 days on different Inspirational Reflections in this book. You should now indicate what insights you got from your reading. List below at least 2 or 3 insights that you got from the Reflections, or information that was reinforced or confirmed.

_____

_____

_____

_____

Day 7 review

You have reflected for the past 6 days on different Inspirational Reflections. To get the best from the material, list below at least 2 areas or particular situations in your life in which you commit to do better.

_____

_____

_____

_____

81. Be conscious of your dreams

Your first challenge of success is to know what it is you want out of life. If you know what you want, then you have a real possibility of getting it. Be conscious of your desires, profess them, and claim the results.

You can with bold assurance manifest your desires, if with confidence you act to accomplish them continuously. One of the secrets of accomplishment is that on a daily basis, constantly affirm your desires firmly and positively. Keep your dream ever present in your mind's eye. You will then find that the people, places and events to support your dream mysteriously appear. Your constant focus on your dreams and desires will attract to your life what is necessary to make your dreams come true.

It always happens that when you are truly focused on your goal, opportunities unexpectedly present themselves to help you realize your goal. This includes support from critical people necessary to facilitate you to achieve your goal. What you put your attention on, grows stronger in your life. Be resolute, keep focus on your passion, and your life will be fulfilling.

82. Be purposeful

You can achieve great things if you have definite purposes in mind. You need to be very clear about what you want to achieve, otherwise you will only achieve it by mere chance. Achievers have purpose. Non-achievers just wish that things will happen; they are not relentless in their pursuits.

Non-achievers have no specific agenda. They go along aimlessly. They have no target to hit.

You may have purpose, but if you are tamed, and subdued by misfortune you cannot achieve greatness. The Universe will not give such a person a clear path. There is such diversity in people and circumstances that there will always be obstacles and blockages on any road you travel.

The measure of a great mind is that it rises above all trials and difficulties. When circumstances and opportunities are not what you intend or expect, take action to live a life of significance.

Your measure of success or greatness is the manner in which you rise above all trials and difficulties. Go out and shine by creating your own favorable circumstances and opportunities. You can do it. It's possible.

83. Be tolerant of others' faults

You can only see through your own mind's eye, due to the limit of your experience and knowledge. But this characteristic of limited vision can be turned to your advantage. You can become more sensitive and charitable to those around you, by reflecting on your own weakness. No one is perfect. We are human, and have all sinned, and come short of the Glory of God.

Although you may perceive the faults of others to be more serious than your own, you must understand that "a fault is a fault." Examine your own faults. They are many, as on many occasions your thoughts, words, and deeds are inappropriate.

When you bare all your faults, you will accept that other people are justified in being upset with you. Conversely, you will appreciate that your faults are as insipid as the faults you observe in others. Being aware of your own weaknesses, will help you to be more tolerant and patient with the faults of others.

Be kind and compassionate towards others, and through the law of attraction, you will receive likewise benefits.

84. Choose to be better

In the next 12 months do you want different and better results than in the last 12 months? Then, pursue a different life design. Make a list of all the things you are REALLY good at. Trim the list to only those things you are passionate about.

From your list of things that you are passionate about choose one that has all these attributes:

- You are truly full of passion for it.
- You can do it on a daily basis, or have the potential to do it daily
- It is the activity that will make your first dollar fastest and easiest.

Follow this resultant activity with consistency and relentlessness and you will be on the road to finding out YOUR WHY, your purpose for living. Do this process, and enjoy a renewed passion for living.

85. Act from love and win the commitment of others

Men and women form naturally into groups and communities. The group will have some common purpose. It may be simply survival or more complex activities such as building a rocket to go to the moon. In pursuing the common purpose of the group, men and women may follow the leader, or the leader may have to order them to do things from a position of status in the structure.

As a leader you have to win the hearts of men and women for them to follow you. To win hearts you have to act from love as opposed to power. Love is defined here as giving of yourself unconditionally, and not counting the cost. Love will give you the empathy needed to relate with others. Love will let you be patient with folly. Love will help you to avoid jealousy. Love will open your wisdom centre. Love will manifest forgiveness.

When you win the hearts of men and women, you win the full actions you desire from them. You also have, either directly or indirectly, access to the full range of their resources.

Day 6 review

You have reflected for the past 5 days on different Inspirational Reflections in this book. You should now indicate what insights you got from your reading. List below at least 2 or 3 insights that you got from the Reflections, or information that was reinforced or confirmed.

_____

_____

_____

_____

Day 7 review

You have reflected for the past 6 days on different Inspirational Reflections. To get the best from the material, list below at least 2 areas or particular situations in your life in which you commit to do better.

_____

_____

_____

_____

86. Beyond the obvious

You have your dreams, hopes, and aspirations, but your life is not blossoming as you would like. I was listening to an mp3 recently, and this comment jumped out at me, "God can only do for you, what He can do THROUGH you." Consistent dedicated action on your part is absolutely necessary.

Be reminded of the concepts, "Don't wait to get it right, just get it going," and "Faith, belief, or desire without action produces nothing."

Whenever you are tempted to say "no" to an opportunity, rethink the situation and determine whether you are merely staying within your comfort zone. I attended a presentation by an international motivator and he expressed the view that when a stranger enters your life and makes a request, keep an open mind, and look for the "yes" opportunity.

This comment struck a cord in me, as recently, being a co-author, I was offered to be in a movie being developed for the co-authors of the book, "A Search for Purpose." I found all the excuses to say "no" instead of "yes." The moral of the story is that you should be a demonstration of who you know you are. Stay strong and courageous!

87. Build your self esteem

Build your self-esteem. How you regard yourself, and how you esteem yourself is your self-esteem. .Apart from problems that are biological in origin, all psychological difficulties can be traced to poor self-esteem. Self-esteem can be described as a feeling of personal competence, combined with a feeling of personal worth.

Your ability to think is the basic source of your competence. The friends you keep, the books you read, what you listen to, and what you view through television, videos, and DVDs greatly influence your thinking. Thus, the company you keep can help you to grow in self-esteem, and expand your capacity for happiness. You will become the average of the five persons you associate with most, and be driven by the books and information you access.

The information you feed your mind should be such as to grow your self-esteem. Persons who never see any good coming from your ideas and plans should be quietly avoided. Talk to people who have had success in their own lives, and they will help you grow in self-esteem. They will endorse your potential of personal competence, and confirm your prospect of happiness.

Develop your mindset for success, by associating with others who have mindsets for success.

88. Design a better life for yourself

You determine your future by the choices you make on an ongoing basis. Personal empowerment becomes possible when you take responsibility for your present condition in life and simultaneously take conscious control of your future.

"As a man thinks in his heart so is he," comments the Scriptures. Thoughts are powerful. If you wish to do or be better than you are now, you have to do some things differently to what you do at present.

Your Personal Empowerment Model can be seen in three steps as follows:

- **Assess:** Where am I now? Look at your current situation. Describe it. Understand what you want to change or modify and what you want to keep, and the reasons for doing so. This is the design, structure and planning stage.
- **Decide:** Having understood your current situation and what you would like changed, decide on the precise nature of the change that you are going to make. Set new goals that will result in the changes you want in your life being accomplished. This is the stage of processing your concepts and vision.
- **Act**: Since you have decided where you wish to go and what you want to do, you can now take relevant action to make your dreams a reality. This is the action and implementation stage.

You have the power to live a life of significance. Use your power and potential wisely.

89. Your decisions of destiny

Your destiny is shaped in the moments of your decisions. When you take your first breath of air outside your mother's womb, your life begins in earnest. The umbilical cord joining you physically with your mother is broken, and your life's process in the outside world begins. You have to seize every moment as you are here today and gone today. Let your every action be significant, and relevant to your dreams.

The most powerful way to live is to take action consistent with what you want to achieve in life. So why do so many persons not take action? Where there is no power of decision, there is no access to action. It is in the moments of decisions that your destiny is shaped.

When you make a decision, there is the natural flow of cause and effect. When you make a decision, you cut off yourself from any other possibility occurring.

Control your life by knowing what things mean to you, taking decisions in keeping with those values, and ensuring that your decisions are consistent with the results you desire.

90. Brighten another's path, and you brighten your own

Life is interdependent. When you serve another person, you contribute to your own development and progress. From a physical standpoint, if you hold a light to brighten another's path, you automatically light the area around you.

You live to make life less difficult for others and when you do so, you make life less difficult for yourself. So often, what you see as a need in another person is a cry to meet a similar need in your own life. By responding to the needs of others you therefore, at a subtle level, soothe your own needs.

When you see the possibility of touching the life of a person in a positive fashion, you bring your experience and training to bear on the situation. When you contribute to another person's consciousness, you also get new and deeper insights into the issues. Your own life, your own consciousness is brightened and lifted.

Thus, light a candle in a person's life rather than fuss about the darkness.

Day 6 review

You have reflected for the past 5 days on different Inspirational Reflections in this book. You should now indicate what insights you got from your reading. List below at least 2 or 3 insights that you got from the Reflections, or information that was reinforced or confirmcd.

_____

_____

_____

_____

Day 7 review

You have reflected for the past 6 days on different Inspirational Reflections. To get the best from the material, list below at least 2 areas or particular situations in your life in which you commit to do better.

_____

_____

_____

_____

Forgiveness builds relationships

91. Don't let others steal your dreams

Have you achieved your heart's desires, or are you on your way to achieving them? You probably have not achieved what you are capable of because friends and family have said that you cannot, or they have not encouraged you to pursue your desire.

Consider that good idea you had, and that goal you wished to achieve, but those persons you told about it, gave you so many reasons why it could not work. This dulled your enthusiasm. You gave up on your dream.

Understand that with faith, effort, and relevant action all things are possible. When you disclose an idea you want to pursue, and you are told by others it is not possible, ignore them. Say to yourself, "I can," and affirm to the person that it's possible, and you can.

Understand that the negative approach by others is done with all good intentions. However, it is based on their impossibility thinking, and fuelled by their own failure to achieve their own desires. Don't listen to them Dare to dream, to believe, and most of all dare to step in faith, and dare to act. You were born to succeed. Get to it!

92. Your thoughts define you

All riches begin in the mind, both material and spiritual. Money flows from an idea. Also, your spiritual progress depends on the ideas in your mind. The quality of your thinking will determine the quality of your future.

From the material standpoint, begin by seeing what others want, and thinking how to provide it at an acceptable price, at a time when it is needed, and at a place that is convenient. People will pay for a product or service they want. Ideas are the levers that move the world.

Why does one person make a fortune and another one remains poor? Essentially, the answer lies in what continuously takes place in the mind. There are two routes, among many others, to making your own fortune. One way is to provide value to the market place by providing a needed good or service. This requires an idea to be developed and effectively executed.

Another route to raising a fortune is through the idea—save and invest first, and spend or consume the balance of your income. The poor spend first and save what is left. The rich first save and invest, then spend what's left. In any event, it is the idea you generate, and not the amount of money saved and invested, that is the starting point of all fortunes.

From the spiritual point of view you need to take the idea and work it for all it is worth. One idea is to love and honor God while you love your neighbor as yourself. To be rich spiritually is to work continuously to be one with God. Use your unique talents to be of service to others, and so fulfill your purpose and destiny.

93. Shine brightly

Your birth was no accident. You are part of a Divine plan for world destiny. You have a unique set of skills and talents that can make a positive difference to your community, and the world. Your challenge is to use your talents wisely. This confronts you squarely when you face difficulties and setbacks in your life.

Each one of us encounters failure, loss of a loved one, financial difficulties and career disappointments. You cannot change the circumstances that have occurred. But you can have a response that permits you to live with positive expectancy.

A key to positive living is to be present to the blessings of what you have rather than focus on what is absent or missing. Let your attitude be one of gratitude. While acknowledging your blessings, you must continue to act with courage and make your best efforts. Taking action daily on a continuous basis to achieve your targets, provides the momentum for success.

The past is a great teacher. However, do not keep it so close to the present that you destroy your future. Viewed properly, what happened in the past—even tragedy—provides a gold mine of information for future success.

You are the star of your show. You can really only change your own disposition. You cannot change others although you may be able to enhance their pool of information to help them take better decisions.

Use your talents to enhance what is happening around you and thereby touch your community, and perhaps the world. Rise above apparent setbacks, and play the music within you. Remember that a diamond cannot be polished without friction. You are a diamond, so use your friction or setbacks to shine brightly.

94. Speak to enhance your success

Life is all around you and there is a natural tendency to express how life occurs for you. Speaking is the predominant way in which you expose who you are. You have views, values, opinions and concerns, and through speech you make them known to others.

One purpose of speaking is to inform others of how you think. Another aspect of speaking is to persuade others to your point of view. It is to your advantage to learn how to speak effectively to enjoy a sense of fulfillment.

Be clear about the results you want when you communicate with others. Writing is critical, but there are many more opportunities to influence others through speaking. Cope with daily communication challenges through polishing your speaking skills.

You need to express your vision and goals clearly and powerfully. The skills to become a more effective communicator can be learned. Great communicators are not all born great. They polish their skills on a continuous basis. You can do this through a combination of reading the books of master communicators, coaching, speaker training, joining a Toastmasters Club or a Dale Carnegie Speaking Program, or any of the many other meaningful communication programs available.

95. Come together, work together and grow together and we will succeed together

No man is an island unto himself. The world is interdependent. From birth the baby forms a relationship with the mother. This is the beginning. The relationship grows and expands into other relationships. There is the immediate family, the extended family, the village, the community, the Nation, the World. All these groupings find a common cause to bind together.

Each person is unique with special traits and characteristics. This creates a challenge to keep together. Settling differences, agreeing to disagree, and showing respect for each other, permit the relationships to blossom. Creating harmony from the diversity allows for progress. Keeping together is one thing, but working together is another matter.

You can keep together with others passively and this will not foster growth. When you work together with others you provide synergy that catapults the group to success. A Group to be effective should have a common design. If the Group keeps and works together to achieve the common purpose this will generate the required success

You should be part of a group, or mastermind setting to take advantage of the synergy that takes place when multifarious talents come together with a common purpose.

Day 6 review

You have reflected for the past 5 days on different Inspirational Reflections in this book. You should now indicate what insights you got from your reading. List below at least 2 or 3 insights that you got from the Reflections, or information that was reinforced or confirmed.

_____

_____

_____

_____

Day 7 review

You have reflected for the past 6 days on different Inspirational Reflections. To get the best from the material, list below at least 2 areas or particular situations in your life in which you commit to do better.

_____

_____

_____

_____

CHAPTER 3: KNOW YOUR DESTINATION

96. Break down your goals into several convenient steps

The mile's journey starts with the first step. When this notion is developed, you get to understand that nothing in life is hard to accomplish. Everything is made up of constituent parts, and the secret of achievement is to segment the problem or opportunity into its constituent parts. Then, master those parts, one by one. For example, your Sunday lunch well laid on the table may appear to be formidable.

There is rice, stewed chicken, macaroni pie, green salad, provisions, vegetables, red beans, and other dishes. However, each dish was prepared separately, and each one planned, step by step. This included some prior preparation the evening before.

Take your particular goal, break it into several steps necessary to achieve success, and master those steps, one after another. For example, you may wish to read six books in the next 12 months. One approach to accomplish such a goal, would be to read five pages every night. This will take you no more than fifteen minutes. Follow the process, and in one month you will have read a book of 150 pages.

97. Dare to face your fear

The vision you have of your future influences greatly what will in fact happen in your life. You fear the unknown. Because the future is uncertain, the temptation is to look at it with eyes of fear.

You ought to look at the uncertainty of the future, as an opportunity for creativity. This is possible if you take the stance that nothing in life is to be feared. It is only to be understood. Relinquish fear by confronting it.

Do what you fear most and it will be the death of that fear. When you take wise action that deals with a fear, you conquer it. When you confront your fear and wrestle with the difficulties they portray, they lose the hold they have on you.

Dare to face the things that scare you, and you open the door to freedom. Look to the future with great expectations, safe in the knowledge that uncertainty has within it the creative seeds of wisdom for your use.

98. Find your "why' of living

Everyone says that you can design your own life. But, somehow your life does not progress in the way you want. Why? On your journey of life there are two main roads you can take. There is the road of least resistance, that most persons take, and so do not get the life they want. Then, there is the alternative to take up challenges in life through steps of faith.

What is easy to be done usually does not provide you with great achievements. You have to stretch yourself to do somewhat more than being merely in your comfort zone. You have to stretch to reach for the stars so you can land on the mountain top. Aim low, and you will remain grounded.

If you wish to design a life of significance, you need to consider these three steps:

- Determine what gives you joy. You may have to go into much activities, and serious action and reflection to identify what really makes you happy. This is one step in finding "your why of living."

- Build your life around that activity that gives you joy.
- Be resolute, consistent and courageous in pursuing the passion you identify. When you follow your passion, the daily distractions that can sabotage you will become irrelevant.

Remember that you were born to be happy. You are engineered for success. You have the seeds of greatness. You have the potential to create the life you want. You can do it It's possible.

99. Give freely of yourself

The best gift you can give to anyone is the gift of yourself. You have unique talents that should not be wasted. When you use your talents, the natural outcome will be to meet some need that requires attention. The life cycle is operated through the principles of giving and receiving. The principle of giving cannot operate unless the principle of receiving is in operation.

Nevertheless, when you give, you get more acclaim than when you receive. Even the Holy Scriptures declare, "It is more blessed to give than to receive." When you give of your talents, you generally provide added value to the people, or the environment, receiving your outpouring.

This explains why when you look at the people who are honored, it is for their giving that they are honored. They give their minds, their skills, their dedication, their physical energies, and their love. Similarly, you must give freely without counting the cost of giving. Give your talents, and you give yourself.

The law of giving is so designed that when you give, you will also receive. You may not receive from the person or event you gave to, or at the time you want to receive, or in the way you want to receive. Nevertheless, the just law of what you sow, you reap applies.

100. Your thoughts s empower you or imprison you

Your whole life is controlled by your thoughts. As you think in your heart so are you. There are two major levels to your thinking. The first level is what you think about yourself—your values, your aspirations, your vision and your goals. This first level establishes how you respond to the challenges of living.

If you have limited beliefs about yourself and your potential, you will be enclosing yourself in a prison erected by those weak thoughts. Thus you have the power through your thoughts to be whatever you want to be, go wherever you want to go, and be the best person that you can possibly be. The second level of thinking is the thoughts you have of other people, and of any situation in which you may find yourself. Be charitable in your thoughts of others, avoid being judgmental, and you will be free.

Know that it is possible to resolve any situation within acceptable limits. Positive thoughts can empower you to reach your full potential. The energy of your thoughts create the various beliefs you have about everything around you. Thus, if you believe you can, you create the basis for its achievement. If you have negative thoughts about yourself, others, and situations, you limit what you can accomplish. Let your thoughts be positive and powerful.

Day 6 review

You have reflected for the past 5 days on different Inspirational Reflections in this book. You should now indicate what insights you got from your reading. List below at least 2 or 3 insights that you got from the Reflections, or information that was reinforced or confirmed.

_____

_____

_____

Day 7 review

You have reflected for the past 6 days on different Inspirational Reflections. To get the best from the material, list below at least 2 areas or particular situations in your life in which you commit to do better.

_____

_____

_____

101. You can achieve your goals

Success means different things to different people. This is due to people having different values, different goals and different expectations. A universal definition of success is the progressive realization of worthwhile goals. Each person's goals are different to the other person's, if only in terms of the time in which they are to be completed, the resources to be applied to achieving them, and the scale, or extent of the results required. If you only stand and stare, you will not achieve your goals.

Two factors that can support the achievement of your goals are:

- It is not sufficient to write your goals, You have to describe them in sufficient detail.
- List the reasons why you want to achieve the goal. The more powerful the reasons, the easier it is to overcome distractions, blocks, and upsets.

You have to act. But it is not merely a matter of doing things right. The things or actions themselves must be the right or appropriate things to be done to accomplish your success. You have to search out success. You have to act with passion at every turn. You have to be relentless in pursuing your goals. It is then, and only then, that you will taste success. You have to go forth bravely, courageously, and with wisdom to claim your success. Go for it.

102. Your feelings influence your destiny

Who you are is determined by your beliefs. You fashion how you feel about your personal contribution to the world around you. Therefore, have a vision of yourself that depicts self-worth, self-esteem, and self-confidence. Believe that you are a worthy person. What you say, and what you do are worthy, and of value.

What someone thinks of you is not really important. You ought not to let someone else's wrong opinion of you become your reality. If you have your own proper values, and a sense of integrity, you will be able to live with yourself.

It is important to understand that we all have different talents, but that does not make one inferior and another superior. Work your talents as best as you can, and that measures your contribution to society. Thus, when someone tries to belittle you, talk down to you, or assume a posture of superiority, do not receive it.

Affirm internally and verbalize that you stand for something of worth, and of great human and spiritual values. You are a worthy person.

103. From knowledge to action and wealth

You must have knowledge to move forward in life. It may be common sense, or more complex knowledge, and most of all there is spiritual knowledge.

Formal knowledge will not necessarily make you rich. There are many highly educated people who are poor. You may have facts and information superior to the average man, but wealth comes from solving problems. University Professors would be millionaires, if wealth came from being able to internalize thousands of bits of information, and rehash them on demand.

Applying your knowledge in a beneficial manner is wisdom. We all have the knowledge that exercise and proper diet are essential for good health. How many of us apply that knowledge.

You need to convert your knowledge into action. Action that provides value and solutions to others, create wealth. You have to create value to others in order to create wealth for yourself.

Seek formal education for the love of learning, and providing the framework to operate in daily living. To generate wealth teach yourself to think creatively, outside the box, and provide solutions for others' needs.

However, consider that you are a spiritual being having a physical experience, as the spirit does not die. Seek to know who you really are, through getting the knowledge of the Spirit.

104. Learn, embrace and focus

What is done is done. When something has happened, you cannot really undo it. You may mitigate it. You may learn from it. You may take some countervailing action. But it is done—finished! When you take or fail to take action, you are acting, at that time, in what you think is your own best interest. When the results of the action are available to you, you may wish you had taken a different position, but the action is already done.

Feeling sorry for yourself will not change the past situation. Have no regrets. Whatever you did, at the time you thought it was in your best interests, although subsequent events may not have worked in your favor. Certainly review the past, and understand what went wrong, so that you do not repeat the same errors in the future.

Another reason to review what has already happened is to enable you to plan effectively your future goals, and to develop the success strategies to accomplish your vision. You use the experience of what has happened to enhance the possibility of succeeding at your next series of actions. Do not dwell on the past, although the present is formed by it, and the future can be informed by it.

Learn from the past, embrace the present, and focus for the future. Despite serious discord in your life now, you can carve out a life of significance. Live in the moment. It's possible.

105. Attention to details generates success

Doing the small things consistently, add up to success. Whatever you need to accomplish is made up of several detailed steps. Consider the day. It is made up of 24 hours. Each hour is made up of 60 minutes and each minute is made up of 60 seconds. Pay attention to the detail of time as the first step in your success.

All success is the result of proper attention being paid to the details of the program necessary for that success. I am reminded of someone in Trinidad who had a franchise to manufacture white face cream. All the samples sent to England for testing proved to be unacceptable quality, as the color of the cream was off-white instead of white. The problem was eventually traced to a detail not being observed.

A part of the process required heating the wax for 60 seconds, but the operator felt that heating for 55 seconds would make no big difference. This change in detail got the final color required to be incorrect. Life is like a puzzle. The sum of the detailed pieces produces success. Be aware of the details required to produce the success you require, and implement them.

Day 6 review

You have reflected for the past 5 days on different Inspirational Reflections in this book. You should now indicate what insights you got from your reading. List below at least 2 or 3 insights that you got from the Reflections, or information that was reinforced or confirmed.

_____

_____

_____

_____

Day 7 review

You have reflected for the past 6 days on different Inspirational Reflections. To get the best from the material, list below at least 2 areas or particular situations in your life in which you commit to do better.

_____

_____

_____

_____

106. Live life fully

You are always reaching for new desires. This is a natural human response. However, if something is not immediately available to you, eliminating an obsessive desire for it, will help you appreciate existing blessings.

Living life fully rests on three main pillars. First, you must know precisely what you want. Second, you must plan, devise success strategies, and take appropriate action to achieve what you want. Third, when you have accomplished your goal, you must enjoy it.

At any moment in time, you have accomplished a great deal in life. Moreover, you have bounteous other blessings. Just being able to see, talk, hear and walk are tremendous blessings in themselves. You can clearly point to many of your other blessings. Pause and check them out now!

Certainly seek to utilize your talents more fully, but recognize your accomplishments, reflect on their goodness, enjoy their fruits, and be conscious of your countless blessings.

In a real sense, the only thing beyond your reach is when you refuse to sacrifice your time, money, energy and relationships to achieve a particular desire. If you decide that something you desire is not reasonably within your reach, eliminate that particular desire to attend to what you are passionate about. What you put your attention on grows stronger in your life. Follow this process to maximize your joy.

107. Serve others to generate your own purpose

Success is a continuous process. It is succeeding at one goal, then another, and another. Success is achieving balance in all the principal areas of your life. People measure your success by their own criteria—money, status, influential friends, material possessions, power and the like. But, you should measure your success by the effectiveness with which you achieve your own goals.

Also, happiness is an internal job. People and things give you pleasure, but your inner responses provide you the fulfillment, and happiness to which you aspire. Your happiness results from being faithful to your own values, while using your talents to provide service and value to others.

Thus, no matter how well you master attainment of your goals, the victory is hollow if you are not happy. You will not be happy if, in the process of using your potential to achieve your goals, you are not of service to others. You cannot take someone else to the mountain-top without going there yourself. Be of service to others, and you generate your own purpose.

108. When opportunity knocks

When I left Queen's Royal College, I was offered a job in the civil service, as well as one in the private sector in the oil industry. The salary of the job in the private sector was double that of the public sector. My mother advised me to take the one in the civil service, as she believed that it offered me more security of tenure. Of course my mother's view was influenced by her own experience of the world depression in the 1930's when hundreds of thousands of employees were laid off world-wide from the private sector.

I did not take advantage of the opportunity to be associated with the modern oil sector. As a dutiful son, I chose the civil service job in 1951. You face this dilemma constantly in your life. Do you opt for the known and safe situation, or do you go boldly forward in the whirlpool of uncertainty? If you wish to go beyond mediocrity you have to take the risk of the unknown when your opportunity knocks.

Years later, in 1970, faced with giving up my job in the public service, and venturing into commercial banking, as the Chief Executive of a commercial bank, I opted for the unknown and uncertain. I resigned from the public service, and lived the life of significance that I desired. I followed my passion to help others solve their financial problems, while I used my talents generously.

By no means be reckless. You must still be logical, cautious, and intuitive, and you must have confidence in yourself, and trust in your God. You are the mastermind and star of your own show. Get to it, and soar as an eagle. You have the power, and it is possible to achieve your dreams.

109. Patience Powers Progress

Today, life is fast paced. However, your progress and success depend on your Patience. In a flash, you can e-mail around the world via the inter-net. In a flash, you get your fast food meal. In a flash, you can speak to anyone overseas, or at home, on your cell phone. This can lead to wanting your other desires and plans to be as quickly satisfied—in a flash!

Natural law as shown by nature, requires a gestation period. For example, you plant tomato seeds today, but the tomato tree does not mature and provide you with tomatoes by the following week. Another example is that despite all modern advances, and new technology, pregnancy normally takes seven to nine months for the birth of a child. In all things, there is a divine gestation period.

Thus, when you have your vision, goals, and desires do not expect them to be achieved overnight. Of course, you do not just sit around and wait. You take all the necessary action during the gestation period to facilitate the eventual outcome. You take relevant action on a consistent, persistent basis. You adopt a mindset to be unstoppable in pursuing your heart's desires.

Persist with pursuing the life you want. There is a difference between being patient and waiting. Patience requires that you do everything that you can to improve your life, while understanding that if you persist, the changes will happen at the right time.

When you wait, you are passive and hope that that things will miraculously occur. Don't sit around and wait; that is unproductive. Work with the power of Patience by doing what you can, day by day, to improve your life. You can be the person you want to be. Go for it. It's possible.

110. Model nature's patience in pursuing your goals

Nature has its own rhythm. Nature is made up of great diversity, and those differences require different gestation periods for events to occur. The cycle for growing cucumbers is different to that for cultivating roses. The so called rising and setting of the sun have their unique cycles.

However, what runs through all of nature is the patience of each strand of nature. Whether it is a shrub, a tree, or an animal, nature is never in a hurry to move to its next stage. Nature has the patience for the mango to move from the blossom of flowers to the full green mango, and then to the ripe mango.

The secret of life is to know what is the gestation period for whatever is the issue and then have the patience to wait for the period to expire. So often you believe that what you desire should be available to you quickly. Develop the patience to wait for the specific period necessary to accomplish whatever particular goal you are pursuing.

Day 6 review

You have reflected for the past 5 days on different Inspirational Reflections in this book. You should now indicate what insights you got from your reading. List below at least 2 or 3 insights that you got from the Reflections, or information that was reinforced or confirmed.

_____

_____

_____

_____

Day 7 review

You have reflected for the past 6 days on different Inspirational Reflections. To get the best from the material, list below at least 2 areas or particular situations in your life in which you commit to do better.

_____

_____

_____

_____

111. The insurmountable situation

Your mind is so constructed that when you get a glimpse of something through an idea or a thought, that possibility can be turned to reality. Your mind has a capacity to find a solution to any problem or opportunity that presents itself.

However, you need to have confidence in yourself and faith in God. You need to have a mind set that looks at the seemingly impossible situation with the following perspective—impossible, difficult, done!

This means that faced with a situation that appears insurmountable, your first reaction may be that this is impossible. Very quickly you must remind yourself that it is not really impossible, but difficult. Flowing from this thought you must take the stance that it may be difficult, but it can be mastered—it can be done.

Underlying this whole approach, you simply have to affirm continuously that, "for a wise person all things are possible, although it may not be wise to do all things."

112. Power to live graciously

Your life is what it is, and your circumstances are what they are. This occurs simply as the result of your thoughts, and choices. Your real challenge is unfolding from within. It is about moving through the fog of the past, and stepping into your personal clarity and power. You have the power to live life graciously. Live it!

Your thoughts shape your face, and give it its peculiar expression. Your thoughts determine the attitude, carriage, and shape of your whole body. The law for beauty and the law for perfect health is the same. Both depend entirely on the state of the kind of thoughts you consistently put out and receive. Your point of growth is always at the centre of your being, not on the surface.

Your daily activities are critical for your life. Do things that bring you joy. This oft times require doing different things until the right one clicks. Don't be discouraged, keep trying, and follow the precept, "never give up" on experiencing a gracious and joyful life. Learn to find ways to relax. It may be through music, social interaction, games, reflection or some other compatible activity.

A wise person once said, "If there is in fact no God, humanity would invent one." A search for your purpose is the connecting link to the Divine. One useful daily refrain could be, "Holy, holy, holy, Lord God Almighty shower me continuously with Divine energy rays."

You have the power to shape the rest of your life. Your mind potential is unlimited with infinite possibilities. Live every moment with joy. Focus on your blessings, and not on what's missing. Be courageous. Live in the moment, with faith, and in hope. I believe in you. You can do it! You can be your best!

113. Press on despite difficulties

Life has many issues which impact you. Very often one of the various values or qualities that you need to follow is in conflict with another value or quality. For example, you may need to be patient, but yet need to be assertive. Courage is a priority quality, and has been defined as the ability to go from failure to failure without losing enthusiasm. Persistence of this kind makes your life a success.

You must pursue your goal in spite of all obstacles. Any of your worthwhile endeavors will have blockages or barriers preventing their achievement. Your life is governed by a vision that is realized through the establishment of a series of goals. All these goals will have upsets and setbacks, of one kind or another. Your ability to persist in the face of all difficulty is thus paramount for your eventual success in life.

Be courageous, persist despite the obstacles or difficulties, and your success in life will be guaranteed.

My own experience has shown that hardships and difficulties are the means by which you grow into more of your potential. Press on! Success is at the end of the tunnel of difficulties.

114. The price of success

Everything you achieve in life has a price attached to it. Nothing in life is really free. When you want something out of life, you have to put something into it. The price may be your time, your energy, your money, your relationships, or some other of your valued resources. If you want to make things better you have to affect the "status quo," and sometimes this can be quite difficult to confront and accomplish.

Through your creativity and updated knowledge, you may see a better way for things to be done. However, you may choose to leave things as they are, so that you do not rock the boat. You remain in your comfort zone. You have to pay a price for that too, as you agonize for failing to make the situation better.

Every advance, every progress you make in life has a price attached to it. Assess every price you have to pay and ensure that the benefits and results, either to yourself or to your environment, are worth the efforts connected to that price.

115. Proper preparation generates success

Have you heard someone say that a particular person is lucky when referring to some success of that person? The comment suggests that the person was not diligently active. In fact, success occurs when preparation meets opportunity.

If you want a job, you must prepare yourself to get the basic requirements for the job. For example, in today's technological age if you did not prepare yourself and become computer literate, whatever job you are aspiring to will probably elude you. When someone else gets the job you will say that this was due to the other person's luck, contact or some other excuse.

If you prepare and the opportunity does not come, the loop is not complete. However, experience has shown that when you prepare and you earnestly set and pursue your goal, unexpected opportunities present themselves. In any event, it is better to be prepared and no opportunity comes your way, than to be unprepared and miss the opportunity that comes your way. Be prepared.

Day 6 review

You have reflected for the past 5 days on different Inspirational Reflections in this book. You should now indicate what insights you got from your reading. List below at least 2 or 3 insights that you got from the Reflections, or information that was reinforced or confirmed.

_____

_____

_____

_____

Day 7 review

You have reflected for the past 6 days on different Inspirational Reflections. To get the best from the material, list below at least 2 areas or particular situations in your life in which you commit to do better.

_____

_____

_____

116. Prosperity is your birthright

In the 1980s while visiting the USA, I met an African American millionaire who was part of a consortium that had just purchased one of the world's leading chocolate companies. Because of our prior business relationships, he offered me a franchise, on concessionary terms, of the newly acquired company to cover distribution of chocolates in Trinidad and Tobago, and the Caribbean.

I politely declined the offer, making the comment that I was not really interested in making money, but in helping the poor and underprivileged in my country. What my millionaire friend then said has remained with me. He said, "Philip, the best way you can help your people is for you not to be poor. You can then help them materially, and not only with motivational words, and great counseling." He made a point to be seriously considered.

You need to understand that there is nothing wrong in being prosperous. What matters is how you gain your prosperity, and how you use it. In fact, creating wealth has to do with how you think about money: the value you put on it. Most people talk themselves out of being rich or wealthy before they ever get started.

They have been sold the belief that there is something wrong with attaining superior financial status. Meanwhile, world-class thinkers, who are usually no more intelligent or educated, are living the lives of their dreams, believing all the while that being rich is more noble than being poor

Don't make the mistake that I made in refusing that chocolate franchise. Remember that Job was one of the richest men of his time, and yet God in Job Ch:2.3 referred to Job as ",,, a perfect and an upright man ..."

Grasp the opportunities when they are presented to you. Change or deepen your mindset. Know that you have talents that can be used for both the spiritual and material prosperity of yourself, and others in deep need. Prosperity is your birthright. Embrace it.

117. Take a stand for yourself

Are you comfortable with your present situation? If you are, perhaps you are not extending yourself beyond your immediate grasp. You are only doing what you know you can comfortably achieve. You are not stepping out of your crease for fear that you will fail. But why waste your talent? Be a man or woman of destiny. Let not your tombstone read, "Here lies John Doe (substitute your name) who is dead, but whose potential was not used up."

To reach your full potential, you have to take a stand for yourself. You have to stand up for what you want out of life. Discover your purpose, exercise your potential, and claim your destiny. Release your internal Tiger—be strong, be bold, be courageous, be cunning, be brave, be alert, be honest, and be compassionate.

If you believe in yourself, and for what you stand, you will soar to a higher level of achievement. Stand up for what you believe in, or be doomed to fall for anything.

118. Pursue your vision relentlessly

Your vision is the target you have for your life. But there are three aspects of your vision that are interrelated:

- What you want to be
- What you have to do, to be
- What you desire to have, to be

What you have to do, and what you desire to have are key parts of your life. However, your only enduring self is what you want to be. Having a beautiful home, taking great vacations, and achieving your other million dollar desires are fantastic, although you are only a temporary custodian of these possessions.

What you achieve in life is not really the important factor. It is whom you become in the process of achieving. If you become what you want to be, then you are in the realm of happiness. When you become who you want to be as a result of achievement, then you can face any difficulty as you have developed the sinews of success to draw upon.

To become what you want to be, set your vision, be courageous, be invincible, and I will see you at the very top. You can live an amazing successful life.

119. Adopt a self-image of success

The image you portray is often more important to your success, than your skills or accomplishments. The impression people get of you depends on how you present yourself through your dress, speech and conduct. How you position yourself in the minds and hearts of others is determined by the image you have of yourself. Your self-image, unknown to you, manifests itself to others looking on.

From birth your mind has been exposed to tremendous negative influences about your competence, and your self-worthiness. Among other things, there was difficulty in writing, trauma of mathematics, drudgery of reading, poor diction, bad spelling, and weak articulation. These all had their damaging negative effects on your self-image.

You need a new positive focus on your life through an acceptance of yourself. Develop a strong abiding belief in the potential of excellence that you are. Your technical skills and past successes are important. However, these pale into insignificance when compared to the capacity within you to shape, and determine your destiny.

You have got to see it in your mind's eye, and truly believe it, to generate your success image. Believe that you can be successful. See yourself as that success, and you will soar like an eagle.

120. Passion, focus, and intensity, manifest your desires

You have desires. Desires are at the level of the mind. To accomplish your desire shift it from the mind to outside the body. This is done by writing down your desire as clearly and specifically as possible. You can then better confront it.

One issue is whether you can commit emotionally to your desire. If the desire is in conflict with your basic values, you have to rethink the desire. Next consider whether the benefits and pleasure of the desire, exceed the pain of pursuing the desire.

Where your emotional commitment to your desire is strong, and there are great benefits and pleasure from pursuing your desire, you will go after your desire intensely. When there is more pain than pleasure in pursuing the desire, the power of its force will be weak, and you will no longer pursue the desire, or you will pursue it with reduced vigor. The greater the passion and intensity, the stronger will be the power that you focus to fulfill your desire.

Day 6 review

You have reflected for the past 5 days on different Inspirational Reflections in this book. You should now indicate what insights you got from your reading. List below at least 2 or 3 insights that you got from the Reflections, or information that was reinforced or confirmed.

_____

_____

_____

_____

Day 7 review

You have reflected for the past 6 days on different Inspirational Reflections. To get the best from the material, list below at least 2 areas or particular situations in your life in which you commit to do better.

_____

_____

_____

_____

Thinking empowers you

121.Take a new step

One bright and beautiful day, a young man, whom I did not know, approached me, and asked whether I still did leadership training. I said "yes." He then asked, "What does a significant leader who has lost his way, do to pick back up the pieces of his life?"

I replied that I assumed he was speaking of himself, and so enquired what caused his downfall? He said that there was a breakdown in his family relationship, and his world came tumbling down, but he is now ready to pick up the pieces.

My suggestion to him was fivefold.

First, learn from your mistake. Avoid repeating it.

Second, clarify your intention, very specifically. Clarity of intention is the first requirement of success.

Third, ensure that you have a passion for what you say you want.

Fourth, take relevant small action steps, on a consistent, regular basis.

Fifth, keep focus and constant review of your results, as what gets measured, gets done.

So there you have it. Apply what is relevant to you. Remember that a goal is a dream with a plot, and an ending.

122. Unfold your greatness

Philosophers from the East make an important point: "you don't need to learn more, you only need to remember what you know." The other side of this concept is that to know something means to honor and observe what you know. So, if you say you know that exercise is good for your health, and you do not exercise, do you really know it?

Your real challenge is unfolding from within. It is about moving through the fog of the past, and stepping into your personal clarity and power. In other words, live your life of significance and greatness. You have the power to do it. My goal is to help you to identify, clarify and resolve your issues in life.

All progress of the individual is based on inner disclosure. Life moves from within, outwards. The germ or vitality is always at the centre, not on the surface. The growth of the tree or plant, comes from the sap within.

Similarly, the individual determines his own position in life, according to the amount of intelligent effort exerted. It is a function of attitude multiplied by skills. For this reason, the majority of people will not work to acquire this Inner Power

Thus, a person will rank among the great or mediocre. You have to make your choice of ranking. Declare war on mediocrity. Make your move to unfold your greatness.

123. Use your power of choice

You have the ability to move your life in the direction you desire. You can be assertive and choose how you want to live. You have the Divine spark that gives you the power to design your life of significance.

Chapter 25 in my third book, "Infinite Possibilities" makes the point this way:

"Oyster or eagle

Two eggs were discussing what they wanted to be when they hatch. One egg said, "I want to be an oyster. I will just lie on the seabed and my needs will be filled. I do not have to plan nor make decisions. The tides and waves will move me around. I will not have to work and exert myself. The sea will provide me with the food I need. What the ocean provides is what I receive, no more, no less. That is the life for me. This is a simple life and I am satisfied with conditions the sea provides."

The other egg said, "That life is not for me, I want to be an eagle. I will have freedom as an eagle. I will hunt for my own food and enjoy the thrill of the hunt. I can explore and be alert. I can see the bigger picture with my vision. I control where I go. No one puts limits on me. As an oyster, brother egg, you are totally controlled by your environment. To enjoy choices as an eagle, I will pay the price required to live like an eagle."

My question to you dear reader is, "Do you want to be an oyster or an eagle?" You have the choice to be laid back, do little and just accept what comes your way. On the other hand, you can impact your future. You can have a vision, dream, plan, develop strategies, and act for the results you want. You can design your own future"

You can be the success you want to be, both spiritually, and materially. Go for it!

124. Use your talents fully

If you have a talent, and you do not use it, you have failed. If you have a talent, and only use part of it, you have partly failed. If you have a talent and learn somehow to use it fully, you have fully succeeded.

When you feel deep down within you the imperative to do what is at hand as well as you possibly can, and your heart murmurs well done, you have done your best. That is accomplishment; that is success.

There are many things that you can do well. However, you have the choice of doing them well or half-heartedly. Do them well, and you will be a success. The other strand of success is to do the things that you are not excellent at, with the best effort you are capable of. Whenever you do your best, in whatever you put your hand to, that is the talent of success.

125. Persistence and commitment ensure success

Think it, commit to it and you will achieve it. The human mind is constructed so that if you think of a possibility, within that thought there resides the seeds for its achievement. Life, being what it is, your path will be strewn with difficulties.

You have many goals but quite a few of them are not achieved—why? The strength of your commitment to any endeavor determines when you will achieve it. When you commit yourself to your goal, every obstacle will be overcome. When you are committed you will find a solution to any blockage of your goal. You will persist in the face of the greatest difficulty. Such focus provides energy and power that resolves all roadblocks, and changes problems into opportunities.

A great commitment to your goal produces a strong desire, and an intense determination that overrides all other distractions that arise. Where you have serious commitment, the achievement of your goal is assured.

Day 6 review

You have reflected for the past 5 days on different Inspirational Reflections in this book. You should now indicate what insights you got from your reading. List below at least 2 or 3 insights that you got from the Reflections, or information that was reinforced or confirmed.

_____

_____

_____

_____

Day 7 review

You have reflected for the past 6 days on different Inspirational Reflections. To get the best from the material, list below at least 2 areas or particular situations in your life in which you commit to do better.

_____

_____

_____

_____

126. Want more in your life?

Do you feel that your life should be more exciting? If so, believe that you have the power to experience fulfilling moments everyday. The steps are fourfold:

- Identify your passion
- Decide what to do with that passion
- Take committed action
- Enjoy the journey

Review your life, and identify what you are passionate about. Consider what it is that gives you joy when you do it. When you are clear on your passion, on what gives you joy, decide on what you can do about it during the next three months. Start a new life with small steps. These small steps consistently followed will build into a huge momentum. You will experience a new feeling of joy and satisfaction.

When you are committed to your passion, you will do what is necessary to honor your passion, not what is convenient. As you proceed on your life's journey, enjoy the ride. Life should be enjoyed. Following your passion is a sure recipe to move you towards expression of your greatness. You can do it. You can live the life that you love. Be steadfast. It's possible!

127. Are you stopping your progress in life?

Your life may not be progressing as you would like. But are you in fact delaying or stopping your own progress? You may not be conscious that you are doing this, so you need to take control of the situation.

You have great vision and creative powers. You have decided what you want. You made plans and devised new strategies to get you where you want to go. However, it is not happening. So what is frustrating you?

Simply put, you are not taking the final step to manifest your dreams. You have to take action consistent with achieving the life you have designed or contemplated. To achieve something new, you have to do some things differently than you did in the past. Come out of your comfort zone, and do things that are uncomfortable, but relevant and appropriate.

Consider what actions you are postponing, but if done will make a significant difference to your life. Then, each day for the next 5 consecutive days take one-step to change the situation. You will create a new sense of accomplishment and empowerment. In 30 days you will be a different better person with a new lease of life. Try it, and soar to greater heights.

128. Why am I alive today?

I dare you to pursue this great challenge. Every day for the next 7 days when you awake, ask yourself, "Why am I alive today?' Then, the first day document what comes to your mind. Repeat the exercise for the next 6 consecutive days as you awake on mornings.

As you proceed with this exercise you will deepen the understanding of your purpose. You will also find that your life becomes more meaningful and fulfilled.

At the end of the 7 days, review what you have discovered as a new angle to your life.

129. You are alive

Today you are awake, so give thanks. Today you opened your eyes, and you are above ground. You are not dead, as so many other persons who were alive yesterday. Thus, be happy. You still have an opportunity to impact your life positively. Therefore, love today and celebrate.

Your condition is not what you would like it to be—so what? You have a chance to fashion your life differently. You can keep on trying to achieve what you believe is valuable and possible. Tomorrow is uncertain. You do not know what life has in store for you. But you should not be afraid, for you survived yesterday.

Yesterday held strong challenges for you. Yesterday seemed that you would not have been able to survive it. You have seen yesterday. You triumphed over yesterday, so you need not fear the unknown, and the unexpected barbs of tomorrow.

In all things, act in love. Be kind. You can transcend all difficulties with the help of God. Go forth with confidence in yourself, and faith in God.

130. Your destination is strewn with rough roads

If you want something you have to really go after it. There are many distractions to overcome on the way to reaching any goal. A key to achievement is persistence. If you really want anything you have to go after it. You have to persist in the face of all difficulties.

If you do not now have something you want, most probably it is because it is not easy to have it. Thus, if you want it, you must be willing to face up to the roughness of the road to obtain it. When you really want something you have to press on, as nothing can take the place of persistence.

Persistence is the ability to face defeat again and again without giving up—to push on in spite of great difficulty. When you are really going after what you want, you convert obstacles into stepping-stones or opportunities. Use the negatives in a manner to support the attainment of your prized goal.

Day 6 review

You have reflected for the past 5 days on different Inspirational Reflections in this book. You should now indicate what insights you got from your reading. List below at least 2 or 3 insights that you got from the Reflections, or information that was reinforced or confirmed.

_____

_____

_____

_____

Day 7 review

You have reflected for the past 6 days on different Inspirational Reflections. To get the best from the material, list below at least 2 areas or particular situations in your life in which you commit to do better.

_____

_____

_____

_____

131. Quiet your mind

The only limit to your accomplishment is in your own mind. Compared to what you can be, you are only half accomplished. You are making use of a small part of your talents, and your physical and mental capacity. There are really no limits to your possibilities. There are more possibilities available than you can imagine, or act upon. When you visualize what is possible, your vision of what you are capable of doing expands. You can then reach out, explore and manifest your potential. You can access your infinite possibilities.

Go within, as one of the techniques you can use, to become aware of your capabilities. Opportunities available to you will surface. Quieting the mind of continuous noise is the trigger to enter the silence within. It is from this silence that creative opportunities spring in the outer world. Enter the silence every day for at least 3 to 6 minutes—morning and evening.

Just find a quiet place, close your eyes, still your thoughts and let your creative intelligence flow. There are many different ways to still your thoughts. One method is simply to observe the rhythm of your breathing.

When you practice this technique of reducing the noise in your mind, you will be surprised at the range of possibilities in your life that will occur to you. Act on the infinite possibilities that are available to you. Move beyond thinking to action.

132. Your actions mould your life

Every action you take has consequences. Things and events do not just happen in your life. They are caused. More importantly, they are caused by your own action, or lack of action. Let your actions be supportive of your good intentions.

Consequences of your actions may not occur immediately. When they do occur you may not relate current events as a consequence of your previous action. For example, to be the best in your field requires rigorous and dedicated training. Unless you take committed action in pursuing your vocation, you cannot become the best. Your health is another classic example. Your eating habits may be unbalanced, and your exercise program non-existent. When in later life you contract diabetes or other ailment, you are reaping consequences of previous actions.

The good news is that your good actions produce good consequences. Your challenge then is always to let your actions be life supporting to yourself, family and environment. In this way, whenever you sup at your banquet of consequences you will have prosperity and happiness. Let your every action be based on goodness, truth and integrity. Your life will then be magnificently designed.

133. Strengthen your vision

"Without a vision the people perish." You need to have a million dollar desire. This may be financial freedom, a house, brilliant career, strong family, good health, spiritual enlightenment, world cruise or any number of your other life's preferences. Your success is grounded in your dream list. Thus, the dream is absolutely necessary, but it is not sufficient for success.

You must take massive consistent relevant action to manifest your dreams. Your dream is definitely "possible," but how "probable" is it? The first requirement is to clarify and list what are your dreams. Otherwise, they will simply remain in your head as dreams, and not move on to be realized. Your dreams are 100% possible. You thought of them, and you have the potential to achieve them. Any glimpse your mind gives you can be grasped, for that is the way the mind works.

The probability of your dreams' realization is between 0% and 100%. The actual probability is dependent on how you set your goals, and the rigor and diligence with which you pursue them. The matrix of success includes how you use your time, the relationships you cultivate, what you read, see and hear, and the constant review of your goals.

There are five major keys to formulate your goals successfully:

- specify and simplify
- written and worthy
- appropriate and attainable
- intentional and important
- target and time driven

Strengthen your vision, soar to great heights, and be unstoppable.

134. Slay procrastination

You have learned a lot in your life. You have great experience. Yet, you are not accomplishing what you can achieve. Why? The answer is simple, but it is not easily achieved. What you know does not make a difference to your life. It is what you do with what you know that determines the life you experience.

Sometime ago I decided to use what I know, but what I had been neglecting. For a long time I have understood that you should not postpone for tomorrow what you can do today. I coach persons about such principles. However, I noticed that things that I should have done weeks before were still outstanding.

I resolved then that for the ensuing 30 days to do ONE thing each day that I had postponed, procrastinated, avoided, or made an excuse for not doing, but if done would make a positive difference to my career, or my life. By the end of the first week it did wonders for taking my on-line business forward.

For the next 30 days do just one thing you have been avoiding that, if done, will make your life or career better. You can rise to the challenge. Do it.

135. The benefits and price of success

There are two aspects of success. One is the price or cost you have to pay to achieve it. The other is the benefits or joys you experience when you succeed in accomplishing your goals.

One opinion is that if you view success as having to pay a price for it, you are missing the point. Success occurs when you achieve your goals. To achieve your goals you are required to have action plans. Anything worth achieving usually requires some sacrifice of your time, relationships, money or some other critical resource under your control.

It is in this sense of sacrifice that early "success gurus" said: you have to pay the price for success. Modern day commentators say that: you should flip the success coin, and look at the enjoyment you will get when your success occurs. In this sense, it is not so much a matter of paying the price, but enjoying the benefits of success.

Thus, focus on the joys and benefits you get from success, and view the sacrifices you have to make as your success investment.

Day 6 review

You have reflected for the past 5 days on different Inspirational Reflections in this book. You should now indicate what insights you got from your reading. List below at least 2 or 3 insights that you got from the Reflections, or information that was reinforced or confirmed.

_____

_____

_____

_____

Day 7 review

You have reflected for the past 6 days on different Inspirational Reflections. To get the best from the material, list below at least 2 areas or particular situations in your life in which you commit to do better.

_____

_____

_____

_____

136. Your struggles facilitate your success

Your struggles and difficulties develop the character that makes you a stronger person to meet future challenges. When you overcome your challenges, you develop the qualities necessary for your best future performance. A young biologist observed that an emperor moth was struggling with considerable difficulty to break out of its cocoon.

Being helpful, the biologist made two small cuts at the side of the opening of the cocoon. Soon, the emperor moth broke free. The young biologist was surprised that the moth's body and wings were out of proportion. The moth could not fly. The moth just stumbled around without soaring elegantly, as emperor moths usually do.

Puzzled, the young biologist drew attention of the phenomenon to an older colleague. His senior explained that the struggle in the cocoon was what developed the wings of the moth. By the young biologist cutting the cocoon, the moth's struggle was insufficient to develop its wings. So too in your life, the trials, the sorrows and your grief are the mortar that bind you together. Obstacles in your pathway make you strong enough to tackle the next opportunity and overcome future obstacles.

Thus, develop an attitude that embraces blocks, barriers and obstacles. To attain success you may have to pass through the valley of despair. It is all part of the journey of achievement. Be persistent and consistent despite apparent setbacks. You must therefore view the various struggles that you have to encounter, as providing the strengthening of your persona of success.

137. Read daily to excel

Your life is precious. With increasing knowledge in today's world, you have to read sensibly to remain relevant. My approach has been to read at least one book in my field of interest every two months.

To achieve this I read for 15 minutes daily. At my speed of reading, this results in 3 to 5 pages daily. Thus, in 2 months I read 180 to 300 pages that is more than the size of most books. Commit to this reading process and in one year I guarantee you amazing results. Count your blessings and live joyously.

138. Everything vibrates, but at different rates

Learn to fit and function in the matrix of nature, and you will have a successful life. You must accept that there is inherent greatness within you. Be in harmony with natural laws, and you will remove negative beliefs you have of yourself. Also, being in such alignment will support achievement of the life you want.

Seven Natural Laws that are under the umbrella of the Great Law that: "Everything is energy" are:

- The Law of Vibration and Attraction
- The Law of Polarity
- The Law of Rhythm
- The Law of Relativity
- The Law of Cause and Effect

- The Law of Gender
- The Law of Perpetual Transmutation of Energy

Everything in the world is made up of energy. The concept is that all matter is energy vibrating at different rates. Every molecule that makes up every bit of matter is filled with great energy. Energy is everywhere, and in everything. There are different types of energy: light, heat, atomic, sound, magnetic and so on. Energy is about potential. In this Reflection, focus is on the Law of Vibration and attraction.

Everything in our universe constantly vibrates and moves. Nothing really rests. With natural eyes you can see your hand, but not radio waves. Differences in vibration of these two elements account for this. Similarly, thoughts and feelings are energy, but you cannot see them with your natural eyes.

You determine your own thoughts and feelings. Your brain is the switch that creates, sends, and receives your energy thoughts. This is a key to getting what you want in life. Producing and sending negative thoughts and feelings, simply materialize similar negativity in your own life. Therefore, if you are unhappy with your life, check what thoughts and feelings you are generating on a consistent basis. They are like a boomerang. They return to connect with you. Be positive. Don't condemn, criticize or complain.

Affirm, congratulate and cherish yourself and others. There is always something good in the worst of us. Be positive to attract positive influences in your life.

139. Habits form your future

The actions you keep repeating that may not appear important, result in either your success or failure. Therefore, be aware of the actions that you are taking on a daily basis. When you do something over and over a habit is formed. The action becomes automatic, and ordinarily you do not examine whether you should continue doing it.

Thus, when you repeat an act over and over you reap a habit. When you sow habits, you reap a character. Sowing character you reap your future. Your future is the outcome of the actions that you have taken in the past. What you put your attention on grows stronger in your life.

Consider success in any field. For example, a scholar has to put attention repeatedly to mastering information of academic and professional subjects. To become the fastest sprinter internationally, you consistently train, have a positive mental attitude, and eat properly. To be a spiritual adept you have to follow assiduously the principles and practices of the pathway. Conversely, being indifferent to how you live on a daily basis, will promote unhappiness, depression and sadness.

Your challenge is to pursue lofty ideals in all areas of your life. Repeat over and over actions that are relevant and wise. Good habits will thus be formed, leading to a meaningful and fulfilling life. At every moment choose right action, and you will soar to great heights like the Eagle.

140. **Working selflessly for others makes love visible**

Work is that activity that gives meaning to life. It is through work that the human spirit finds expression. One Sage put it this way, "to work is to worship." Also, it is by working that you can give service to others, while giving expression to your great talents.

Through work you provide for your family, while supporting others to provide for their families. It is this mutual meeting of your needs and the needs of those around you that elevates work to love. Divine love is awesome. It is kind, long suffering, not jealous, thinks no evil, rejoices in the truth, and endures all things. You work to be a success, and love is perhaps the most important ingredient of success.

Without love your life is empty. When you do work for it's own sake—unconditionally—you are manifesting that great subtle quality of love. Work with the intention of giving of your best and of being of maximum help to others and you will have made love become visible.

Day 6 review

You have reflected for the past 5 days on different Inspirational Reflections in this book. You should now indicate what insights you got from your reading. List below at least 2 or 3 insights that you got from the Reflections, or information that was reinforced or confirmed.

_____

_____

_____

_____

Day 7 review

You have reflected for the past 6 days on different Inspirational Reflections. To get the best from the material, list below at least 2 areas or particular situations in your life in which you commit to do better.

_____

_____

_____

_____

141. Achieve through small regular steps

Start where you are with what you have, and do what little you can. Quite often you are waiting on the right time, and on perfect circumstances. This means you will never get going. Start where you are right now with what you have. Take little step by little step, and keep the momentum going.

A watermelon cannot be eaten in one bite. You can eat the whole watermelon, but you have to eat it one bite at a time. If you looked at the large size of the watermelon, and gave up because of the small size of your mouth, this would be tragic. It is the same with life. The objective may seem large, but it can be broken up into small parts. Do whatever little you can. The tap dripping drop by drop into the bucket at first does not seem much, but in a short while the drops fill the bucket.

Thus, you will be making the greatest of all mistakes if you do nothing about your condition in life. Do something small towards your goal although it does not appear at first sight to be significant. Do what you can. The mile's journey starts with the first step. Start where you are, with what you have, and do what little you can. Life is hard, but inch-by-inch life is a cinch.

142. Success requires activity

Happiness occurs as a result of your being in activity rather than being idle. Activity is the oil that keeps the wheel of life from becoming rusty and jammed. Your body itself gives a clue to the importance of activity. Blood is active throughout your body. When the activity or circulation of the blood is interrupted, the body does not function at its best.

When there is absolutely no activity of the blood, it is a sign that death has occurred. Similarly, when there is no activity in your life, you experience dullness and boredom. The activities of human beings operate on four levels: the physical, emotional, psychological and spiritual.

Activity is demonstrated on the outer through building something, writing, teaching, gardening or other physical activity. When there is relevant activity, you experience an inner feeling of joy, accomplishment and happiness. If you want to be really happy, avoid being idle.

Use your talents in some worthwhile activity that inspires you and contributes to your environment. Have a big dream that also contributes to others, and use your talents in their service. This exchange of energy will benefit you as well as others, and the environment. Be active.

143. Your desired results

Establish what you want to achieve in life and then act to produce the results. To bring about desired right results in your life, right efforts have to be made by you. If your tremendous efforts are not the correct ones, your expected results will not occur.

Put emphasis on the right things that will deliver the life you believe to be right. If what you hoped for is not achieved, you would have done your best in the circumstances. Your life should be so balanced that any disappointment would not frustrate you for a prolonged period.

No matter what misfortune overtakes you, there still remains a whole magnificent man or woman. Hope springs eternal, so any stripping of your hope is only temporary. The essence of greatness is to know that virtue and manifested right actions are enough. Be joyous and let the spirit of peace and right action be ever present in your life.

144. Act in love

Your life is made up of action upon action. Life is dynamic. You either grow or decline with every act you do, or thought you think. Whatever you do has as its basis love or hate, selflessness or indifference, power or service. When you do something, let it be in love for the benefit of others and your community.

Among its many characteristics, Love is kind, patient, just, forgiving, and not jealous. The golden rule of living is "love your neighbor as yourself". This means that you must have self-love and not selfishly put yourself first, second, third, last and also for lagniappe.

It also means that the love you have for yourself has to be extended to others. When you live a life of love rather than a life of exercising power, you open up the possibilities of becoming the best that you can be. You release the potential of your talents. Do all things with love, and you will experience untold joy and happiness in your life.

145. Your life is created decision by decision

If you are sitting in your drawing room and you are considering whether you should go outside in the yard, what is the issue? The first order of business is that you have to decide that you are going outside. You are not going to remain sitting in the drawing room. That first mental step transmits messages to your muscles and nervous system.

You get up from the chair and start walking towards the door. Nothing happens with your bodily movements until that first step of deciding that you are not staying sitting in the drawing room. This same principle applies to other areas in your life. If you are at a particular point, and you want to get to another point, you have to decide on that movement. Decision is the key to success. Decision is the pathway from shifting from one condition that you are in, to any other condition that you want.

Making one decision by itself oft times does not get the job done. You have to make a series of decisions, virtually day by day, to accomplish worthwhile goals.

Day 6 review

You have reflected for the past 5 days on different Inspirational Reflections in this book. You should now indicate what insights you got from your reading. List below at least 2 or 3 insights that you got from the Reflections, or information that was reinforced or confirmed.

_____

_____

_____

_____

Day 7 review

You have reflected for the past 6 days on different Inspirational Reflections. To get the best from the material, list below at least 2 areas or particular situations in your life in which you commit to do better.

_____

_____

_____

_____

Chapter 4: You are the Star of your Show

146. Experiment with achievement

Let's try something new to achieve your goals. Decide on a goal you want that is not easily achievable. Before you read on, get a bit of paper or use your computer, and record it. Be specific, set a time for its achievement and state it in measurable terms. It must not be an impossible goal, but it must stretch you.

Find an emotional reason to achieve the goal. If you do not achieve the goal, you must pay a penalty. The penalty for not achieving the goal must really hurt you. It must be something that you will detest doing, or detest losing. What will constitute this self-activated emotional blackmail will differ from person to person.

For example, I avoid being in the company of toxic people for any prolonged period. Toxic people continuously complain, criticize and condemn. Thus, my penalty may be spending two hours per day for fourteen days with toxic people. This penalty will help me eliminate the excuses for not pursuing my goal.

The principle is that the fear of loss is always greater than the desire for gain. Thus, a desire to gain a new Lexus car, may not be powerful enough to motivate you. However, if not achieving your goal means loss of your house, this may be different.

If it is difficult to set a challenging goal, these ideas may trigger your thinking:

- Wake up every morning two hours earlier to work on some specific goal.
* Have no confrontation with your loved one for thirty consecutive days.
* Walk two miles every day.
* Do not read the daily newspaper or turn off the television for 30 days.
* Read a motivational or self-help book 30 minutes every day, until you finish reading the book, or listen to any motivational tape for 30 minutes every day for 30 days.

You should have got some ideas for your experiment by now.

The next stage of the exercise is the fun part. Decide on something that will really pain you to do. It must be a serious discomfort for you to do it, or not do it. That's the price you have to pay if you do not achieve your goal.

You must be fair to yourself. Your goal must be a serious stretch for you. The penalty for not achieving it must be a horrendous emotional experience for you. This technique provides an ongoing system to keep you on track with your commitments. It gets rid of the many excuses you make for non-achievement of your goal. Select someone with whom you will share this experiment, and let the person monitor your progress with the experiment.

147. Work your dream

Effort that is directed to some specific end becomes work, and its attainment may produce joy and happiness. Work is defined in the

Chambers 20th Century dictionary as "effort directed to an end". Human nature is such that it is difficult to exist without being involved in some form of activity.

Persons often define work to mean narrowly, only those activities that result in some kind of quantifiable monetary return. The Chambers dictionary widens the concept of work to any "effort directed to an end". The key is that the effort must not be aimless but directed to an end. There must be purpose in your activity.

When there is purpose, and an objective to be obtained by your activity, you have the makings for joy and happiness in your life. When you know why you are doing something, you have the possibility of being joyful in doing it.

The stronger your reasons for action, the easier you will overcome obstacles. Powerful reasons for doing something, provide powerful motivation for enduring to the end. When you actually accomplish the end you had in mind, then work provides you with happiness. To produce effort with an end in mind provides the possibility of experiencing joy and happiness. The ball is now in your Court. Take new action, new initiatives, and follow your dream.

148. Focus and wisely manage your daily activities

Life has two principal areas that determine what becomes of you. The first area is the focus on your vision. There are many distractions in life, and you have to determine what is important in your life. You have to choose the career, and the spiritual or religious principles that are important to you. You have to choose the friends that are important to help you attain your goals. You have to choose the types of food that are important for a healthy body.

At every moment in time there are so many competing elements that you consistently have to keep in mind those things that are important to achieving your vision. Do the things that are primary and critical to accomplishing your goals, rather than those things that are urgent but secondary.

The second area that governs life is the time selector. You have only 24 hours in each day, and at the end of each day, those 24 hours are lost forever. The key to accomplish your life's ambition thus depends on how well you use your time to select, and do those things that are important to you. The wise manner in which you manage your daily activities determines your success. What you place your attention on assiduously becomes manifested. Keep your focus, and wisely manage your daily activities, and you will be handsomely rewarded.

149. Action versus thinking

The conventional wisdom is that through good thinking you may generate good action. An alternative view is that you can more easily act yourself into good thinking, than think yourself into good action.

The point is that action is the direct route to success. You can generate your success by making some wise, conscious choices that lead to positive actions. Action produces results, and massive actions generate massive results. Follow this formula to catapult your success:

- Take responsibility for what you do. Do not blame others for your life.
- Take prompt decisions.
- Take the necessary persistent action consistent with the results you want.

Rewind the video of your life. Are you happy with what's going on in your life? Do you lead a fulfilling life? Are you doing what you want to do? Are you materially wealthy, but spiritually poor? Are you spiritually balanced, but materially poor? Are you and your other significant one growing together, or growing apart? Are your relationships working? Are you satisfied with the lifestyle you have?

The kernel of being human is the capacity to desire personal growth, and to make appropriate choices. Change may be inevitable, but growth is optional. The start of increased happiness is deep acceptance of where you are right now.

Do not beat yourself for what you see in the mirror. Have compassion for yourself. You have done the very best that was humanly possible for you at the time. You are alive and there is still possibility. It is only on death that there is no more possibility in this life. Be courageous and strive to live your dreams powerfully. You can do it.

150. Your web of ideas determines your success or failure

When you are born, your conscious mind comes with a relatively clean slate of information. While in your mother's womb, and after birth into this world, you are exposed to sounds, actions of others, and a myriad of emotional and physical experiences. All these impulses are implanted in the data base of your mental computer, and form the store of information available to you throughout life.

From this you develop your core values, your plans, your aspirations, and your whole vision and mission for life. In a specific instance you may be conscious of the idea that is governing your particular situation, but there are many cases in which you are not really conscious. For example, you may lack self-confidence, but not realize that this is occurring because as a child you have been called stupid, or some variant of this, so often.

Your own web of ideas, determine the significance that your life takes. You create your own life, and attract your own prosperity or difficulties by the continuous set of ideas that you use to govern you. Virtually every action you take is governed by a belief concerning that action. Your belief system, on the whole, maps out the person that you will become. Examine your belief system for credibility, truth, relevance, and applicability.

Day 6 review

You have reflected for the past 5 days on different Inspirational Reflections in this book. You should now indicate what insights you got from your reading. List below at least 2 or 3 insights that you got from the Reflections, or information that was reinforced or confirmed.

_____

_____

_____

_____

Day 7 review

You have reflected for the past 6 days on different Inspirational Reflections. To get the best from the material, list below at least 2 areas or particular situations in your life in which you commit to do better.

_____

_____

_____

_____

Recognize your brilliance

151. Pursue your ideas to be your best

You have great potential that you do not use. You can do much more than you are doing now. Ideas flow freely, but you do not follow up on them. Your strength is your weakness. You have so many good thoughts passing through your mind, but you do not fully develop any. An avalanche of ideas is the enemy of success. When you have many competing ideas you do not bring focus to the table.

What's the solution? Pick two or three of the best ideas that you have for your progress, and success. Then choose the one that you consider of highest priority for you.

Focus on that top priority item for six months, and you will soar to new great heights. Plan for its achievement. Take action every day towards its achievement Develop new strategies. Take massive, consistent, relevant action.

What you put your attention on grows stronger in your life. You can achieve your dream. Put your attention on what you intend to accomplish, and you will realize your intention. You have the capacity to live your dreams powerfully. Go for it, and live your greatness.

152. Break down your major goal into sub-goals

Whatever you want to achieve has to be accomplished one small step at a time. The particular step may be small in relation to your goal, but it is important to maintain the momentum to achieve success.

This concept helped me to write my third book. I focused on the title and sub-title. This was a small step but important. I took the step of drafting the constituent Parts of the book. Moreover, I took one small step every day to write five hundred words and so completed the first draft 90 days after my work plan was outlined. Inch by inch you achieve every goal.

You can apply this process of focus to anything that you really want to achieve. It requires commitment. It requires ferocious attention, which eliminates or overcomes all distractions. It requires you to be passionate, and full of enthusiasm about your desire. It can be done if you want it badly enough.

There are three kinds of people:

- People who make things happen
- People who watch things happen
- People who ask, "what has happened?

Be a person who makes things happen. Go for your dreams. It's possible.

153. Strive for better relationships

Your relationships determine the quality of your life. The good news is that you can always build better relationships, if you really want to. You have the possibility to affect positively the persons with whom you interact. Accept the responsibility for making your relationships work. Express kindness with no strings attached. Be willing to give and receive without keeping score.

Understanding yourself is the first principle of personal growth. I got an insight why my relationships were not harmonious. This awakening happened to me when I became aware of my narrow and limited views. I wanted things my way, or no way at all, because, " I was right." Do not fall into this trap of self-righteousness.

Love should be the basis for all types of relationships. Love in this context is not physical attraction. It is the extraordinary feeling of affection without asking or expecting anything in return. It is your gift of drawing out the greatness in others. It is dealing with persons without finely focusing on the cost, while providing service, empathy and truth.

There are two action steps that can improve your relationships. First, encourage others to give you feedback on yourself, while initially being neutral to their feedback. Listen to what they have to say, rather than defend or justify your positions. There will be a time later on when you can reflect and assess.

Second, continually look for opportunities to give positive feedback, praise and encouragement. Take every opportunity to make people feel better about themselves, and what they do. However, this must be done with integrity and be specific. Dare to reach for amazingly better relationships. It starts with you. It is your responsibility.

154. Activate your personal efforts

When circumstances are not what you want, a great person goes out and creates required favorable circumstances. Your environment does not necessarily determine what you can achieve. Where there is no beaten path, you can blaze and leave a trail. You do not accomplish things by so called luck or chance. Luck is preparation meeting opportunity. This means that your favorable circumstance is dependent on your prior preparation, permitting you to grasp opportunity.

Others can best help you, if you have already helped yourself. Other persons can be better able to exercise discretion in your favor, if you have done the appropriate work already.

Your achievement and success depend on the personal effort, commitment and skill you apply to your lifestyle. Decide today on what you really want in life, and go after it relentlessly. You can live your dreams powerfully

155. Your value increases, when you do more than is expected

In our Western system, the market place selects and allocates resources. What happens to you in our economic system, or where you stand on the financial ladder is a direct function of the value the market place perceives you to be.

You may be a valuable brother, a valuable member of your church, a valuable friend or valuable in the sight of God. However, what you earn or what financial reward you get depends on the value that the market-place perceives you to be.

One method of taking up your value in the market place is doing more than is legally or organizationally required of you. This extends to doing more than is required of you when you are giving your services free of charge. When you do more than is required or expected of you, your value increases.

The person who just gets by in life is one who does just sufficient so that his/her services are not terminated. Such a person is also paid just enough not to give up the job. Thus, always do more than is required of you to become an outstanding success. Become a person of value to others.

Day 6 review

You have reflected for the past 5 days on different Inspirational Reflections in this book. You should now indicate what insights you got from your reading. List below at least 2 or 3 insights that you got from the Reflections, or information that was reinforced or confirmed.

_____

_____

_____

_____

Day 7 review

You have reflected for the past 6 days on different Inspirational Reflections. To get the best from the material, list below at least 2 areas or particular situations in your life in which you commit to do better.

_____

_____

_____

_____

156. Your values govern your choices

Your choices are governed by your values. Your values are shaped by your thoughts. Thoughts produce action. Actions produce habits. Habits produce your life. It is a circle. Whenever a negative thought occurs to you, become aware of it and replace it with a positive thought.

You alone have the responsibility to shape your life. When you understand this, you know that nothing, and no one, can deny your greatness. You advance your cause or hold back yourself. Persist in shifting personal responsibility to someone else, and you will not discover the meaning of your own life.

So how can you bring God into the equation of life? Simply, pray as if everything depended on God; and act as if everything depended on you. In other words, discover your purpose in life, and use your unique talents to provide the service you can best provide.

Your human inheritance is your freedom to choose. At every moment you make choices, either consciously or unconsciously. It is the one gift that no one can take from you. Likewise you have to accept the responsibility for the outcome of your choices.

Who you are today, and what will become of you tomorrow flow from the choices you make. Your choices are triggered by your thoughts. Let positive expectancy reign in your life. You can do it!

157. How are you responding to life

You have the power to decide how you are going to respond to life and, by implication, how the next 12 months will unfold for you. You have not achieved all your goals planed for the past 12 months, but don't be dismayed. You can sow seeds in the next 30 days that can provide miracles for your future.

What one thing you keep postponing, that acted upon would produce significant improvement in your life. This could be in your work career or your personal life. Commit this moment to identify it, and take at least 3 action (not thinking) steps (no matter how small) between now, and the next 30 days. Take these 3 action steps, follow the time worn adage, "never, never, never give up," and you will be on your way to achieving your million dollar desires.

158. A breakthrough in your life

The first month of the next 12 months has gone. What are your expectations for the ensuing year? Set one new challenging goal, and go after it massively. Determine what you can do to make your life joyous, exciting and fulfilling. Consider what it is that you are very good at doing, and plan your priority goal in that area.

Ask the question, "If I achieve the results of this goal, what difference will it make to my life?" The answer will tell you whether it provides the excitement, passion and happiness that you want.

Commit to the life you want, focus and take the necessary action that is required to make a breakthrough in your life.

159. Set your sails for success

Proceed in your life in the right direction, if you want to get to your correct destination. Success in life requires you to take appropriate consistent action. If you remain where you are, without movement, there will be no progress in your life. The analogy of a ship is instructive.

If your ship is in port at anchor, its power and potential are not operative. The ship has the ability to conquer oceans. It can also deliver tremendous amounts of goods and people from one place to another. But the value of the ship is in its sailing to get from one port to another, and not remaining in harbor. If the ship lifts anchor but does not set a course, the ship will merely drift. So too in life, you have to set your sail to reach your destination.

You must know where you are going, not merely be swept along with distractions or unexpected events. Your sail represents the strategies you must follow to get what you desire in all areas of life. Your strategies are what you will do differently to get you to your new desired position. Success occurs through setting your sail correctly, and diligently pursuing the life you earnestly desire.

160. Take care of trifles and you settle your life's design

The human being's eternal striving for perfection has been referred to as the worst disease of the mind. It is the nature of human beings to want more and more. They are not satisfied with their accomplishments. They always believe that they can climb a higher mountain. This is not surprising as Jesus himself said "Be ye perfect, as I am perfect." Thus, being human, perfection will elude you.

Perfection requires such effort, knowledge and wisdom that it is no trifle. Perfection means doing something, or being something without any flaws. Any activity, or the creation of anything, has a system or structure that makes that activity or creation possible.

Examine a simple leaf from any tree and observe the elements of that leaf. Individually, the elements all appear trifling: There is the sap, the stem, the veins, the lobe, tip and chloroplast. But together they make the perfection necessary to complete the leaf. So if you are striving for perfection ensure that you take care of the trifles, for without conquering the trifles there is no success. The adage goes, "perfection is no trifle, but trifles make perfection."

Day 6 review

You have reflected for the past 5 days on different Inspirational Reflections in this book. You should now indicate what insights you got from your reading. List below at least 2 or 3 insights that you got from the Reflections, or information that was reinforced or confirmed.

_____

_____

_____

_____

Day 7 review

You have reflected for the past 6 days on different Inspirational Reflections. To get the best from the material, list below at least 2 areas or particular situations in your life in which you commit to do better.

_____

_____

_____

_____

161. Is a Lifestyle Coach necessary?

Do you want a breakthrough in your life? Make a reality check to determine whether it may beneficial to engage a Lifestyle Coach. Consider whether you fit into any of these categories:

- Your life feels unbalanced. You are putting a lot of time and energy into things that are not of top importance.
- You are already successful, yet feel that there should be more to life.
- You are talented but feel that you are not getting where you want to go.
- You are in a major life transition, and feeling that there are no signposts to guide you.
- You are facing important choices that are difficult to make.
- You are working at a job that makes you feel miserable and unfulfilled.
- You often feel unable to act and speak according to your true values and beliefs.
- You sometimes feel that no one cares for you and you have need for a confidant.
- When you have an exciting idea, people you share it with are negative and discourage your enthusiasm.

Answering "yes" to three or more of the situations above, suggests your need for a coach. Many people with problems listed above who have hired a coach, report tremendous positive results. I can confirm being in many of the situations above, and can attest benefits of coaching. Moreover, I am a Lifestyle Coach myself.

Coaching sessions take you on your journey of success and balance in your life. Do you wish to change something in your life? It may relate to your finances, relationships, career, health, spirituality, or other significant aspect of your life. Rise to the challenge of living your greatness.

Take the plunge if you feel trapped in any of these conditions and talk with a coach. I assure you that it would be helpful. I really believe a coach can help you to live the life you want. You may be able to solve these problems on your own, and that is great. If you want to deal with them more quickly and powerfully than by yourself, coaching is available. There are many competent Lifestyle Coaches that you can choose from.

162. You are the pivot for your success

You have had great desires to have an amazing life but it just has not happened. Why is this? You have the vision for your destiny. You set goals. You develop new strategies and take new action. Yet still, your life is not occurring as you expected.

Assume that you have clarity of intention, and you are passionate about your dreams. The reality of living is that there are many distractions to shift your focus from your dreams. You may also have family, friends and associates who wish you well. Yet still, you are not experiencing the manifestation of your dreams.

The basic premise must be that "if it is to be, it is up to me." In the end, dreams do not happen, they are caused. An overriding principle is that YOU must be willing to do what is necessary to achieve the results. If you want to achieve the dreams of your life, you need to take appropriate massive relevant action. You cannot achieve your dreams without taking the serious action necessary for activation.

Manifestation of your dreams require effort, persistence and commitment equally consistent with the magnitude of the dreams.

163. Your experiences fashion your life

Every experience you encounter exposes a lesson in life that is essential for your personal growth. Your life is governed by a grand design. Every experience is part of the puzzle for your personal growth. Each experience you pass through has a purpose, and exposes a lesson in life essential for you to learn. If you do not learn that lesson, it will recur in another form. You are doomed to repeat the experience until you learn the lesson.

Life is about removing the curtain that blocks the Light from your life. The curtain is your ego. You must overcome the passions of the mind to awaken the Divine spark within you. The passions of the mind are anger, lust, attachment, greed and vanity.

Overcoming attachment is the greatest challenge. Attachment to money, loved ones, career or anything that absorbs your attention fully, and passionately.

An experience that may seem as a mistake, or a failure provides you with a data base to avoid that error in the future. Thus, for each experience you encounter you should have an enquiring attitude. That is, what lesson is the Universe trying to teach me through this experience? Everything in life is interconnected in some way. What you experience today gives you wisdom for tomorrow. Pressure on coal converts it to diamond. Similarly, each experience brings you nearer to understand your Higher Self.

164. Your life 5 years from now

Do you want to know what your life will look like in 5 years' time? One view is that your life will look like the average of the lives of the 5 persons you now associate with most. Wow! What a thought to reflect on. Put simply, you are greatly influenced by the constant energy flowing around you. If the persons who most impact on your life are negative, or non-nurturing, or non-affirming you are in a desolate place. Persons around you should first of all have a personal vision, otherwise they cannot support your vision.

It is not always possible to eliminate completely persons who block or drain your energy and ambitions. It may be a family member, close friend, or a work companion. However, in such cases you reduce to a minimum the time you spend with them. Then, replace that time with other persons who have a mind set similar to your own.

A useful approach is to have a network of persons who can provide you with five critical attributes:

- A confidant or committed listener to whom you can disclose your inner self. This is the most difficult person to select, as it requires the person to be totally confidential and discreet. A wrong choice of confidant has the potential to destroy your life.
- A person who critiques or analyses constructively
- Someone to inspire or motivate you
- A possibility thinker who takes you outside your comfort zone, and shows you other possibilities
- A person with technical, or expert skills in the particular area of pursuit.

You will not be able to get one person who can provide all the required attributes outlined above. Carefully select three to five persons and let them know the roles you would wish them to play in your life. Also, the technical or expert person may have to change from time to time depending on the project you are pursuing. Live fully and wisely. It is your birthright.

165. Pursue new possibilities to find a better way

Economics can be defined in many ways. One of the definitions places focus on finding the best way to allocate scarce resources that have alternative uses. This is a useful approach, since generally you do not have everything you want in life.

The underlying concept is that as individual scarcity is the norm, there is an optimum way to do anything. The challenge is to find a way to do it better. Another way to express it is: "with the same input, create more output, or for the same output use less input."

Life is about using and developing your creativity to best advantage in all areas. How do you find a better way to do what you are doing now? The Sages say that whatever you focus on grows stronger in your life. So put what you are doing under the microscope. This relentless attention will open up new possibilities. Open your mind to these new possibilities and you will find a better way.

Day 6 review

You have reflected for the past 5 days on different Inspirational Reflections in this book. You should now indicate what insights you got from your reading. List below at least 2 or 3 insights that you got from the Reflections, or information that was reinforced or confirmed.

_____

_____

_____

_____

Day 7 review

You have reflected for the past 6 days on different Inspirational Reflections. To get the best from the material, list below at least 2 areas or particular situations in your life in which you commit to do better.

_____

_____

_____

_____

166. Act on your knowledge

Facts or data that are analyzed and structured become information. Information that is understood or acted upon becomes knowledge. Knowledge that is applied creatively and appropriately becomes wisdom. Wisdom is the glue that bonds success.

It is not sufficient to know something; you must be wise with that knowledge. To be successful in life or to accomplish worthwhile goals you need to make wise decisions. The best decisions occur when you apply your knowledge with common sense, logic and intuition. The technology available in this information age permits unbelievable storage, retrieval and display. There is thus every reason for you to be well informed. However, you must understand that having the best information in itself is not sufficient.

Knowledge arising from that information does not necessarily make a difference to your life. It is what you do with the knowledge that is the determining factor. For example, you may have the knowledge that a proper diet, exercise and adequate rest are crucial to good health. But, you may not use that information wisely. It is not sufficient to know something. You must act with sensitivity and astuteness on that knowledge. You will then achieve what you want from life.

167. Is your past haunting you?

Are you stuck in the past? Do you find that you keep thinking about what went wrong eons ago? Are you still regretting that broken relationship or lost opportunity? If you keep drifting in the dream of what happened some time ago, you are similar to millions the world over.

However, you can break the chains of the past. Certainly learn the lessons the past provide, so that they are not repeated. But move on. A Lifestyle Coaching Program will support you to learn from the past, but focus on the present to deliver the future life you want.

Are you ready to begin living the life you always wanted? Are you ready to enjoy more success and happiness? Are you ready to be more confident? Then enroll in my six or twelve month personal success coaching program. It can be done by e-mail and telephone coaching, if it is not convenient for you to meet with me personally on one-on-one confidential sessions.

If you are unable to release the past, then you can now have the power to change that. Your mind produces the thoughts, and you are in control of your mind. I hope so! Move forward by giving your mind new powerful thoughts to ponder. Find your passion and live it. Through my coaching program, you can soar to amazing new heights of success. Try it, you may be happily surprised.

Don't put off investing in yourself for your future success. Call (868) 487-9224, or e-mail me at philipgrochford@hotmail.com today for information on starting your new journey of living the life you want.

168. Fulfill your desires

What is your life about? Contemplate what is happening to you. Looked at squarely, your life is about desire. You have the urge to fulfill several desires. Desire for happiness, security, financial freedom, successful children, loving relationships, good health, spiritual growth and many other things. The journey of life is desire.

The important point is to be clear on your desires, and not have a hazy notion. After clarity, prioritize your desires. You have limited time, money and other resources. You cannot accomplish all your desires simultaneously—so prioritize them.

Develop strategies to deliver your desires. For example desire for physical fitness requires strategies of doctor's visits, and following exercise and diet routines. Then take action, massive action to deliver your desires.

Finally, review regularly your results and modify strategies and actions as necessary. Your life is your own. Claim it through intelligent positive actions consistent with your desires.

169. Have a better vision for your life

Boost your life, and get amazing results. At present you have the most experience in your life and the highest skill set and training. This means that you can use your accumulated talents to get unusual breakthrough results in the upcoming period. Of course, you have to do some new things, and reinforce what has given you good results.

These are some elements to consider:

- Invest in yourself to boost your natural talents
- Reduce your limiting beliefs
- Change the habits that sabotage your dreams
- Establish a structure of priority daily activities

Your mind is as enduring as your body, so spend as much on your mind as on your body. How well did you follow this principle during the last 5 years.

You are limited only by what you think you can do, or cannot do. Open your thinking to the notion that all things are possible because of your great potential, and wonderfully engineered creation.

Some of your habits do not support what you want to achieve in life. Identify them, and root them out. Also, let your daily activities be done on a priority basis, to avoid wasted time that cannot be recovered.

As you start the first day of your new life, follow this great program in this Reflection to make the breakthrough in your life that you so desire.

170. What you expect with confidence tends to materialize

One of the seven mental laws is the law of expectations, which states that you do not get what you want, but you get what you expect. What you expect with confidence tends to come true. This relates to matters within your control, not fantasy such as winning the electronic lottery.

Things are brought into existence by the thoughts that your mind generates. Two forces are working. First, the more you think about something and focus on it, the more likely you are going to see ways and means to materialize your thoughts. You will generate plans and actions to accomplish what you visualize.

At another level, when you keep on expecting things to happen, you set up a chain of vibrations to give effect to your thoughts. To feel in your innermost being that you will achieve what you set out to do, opens the door to miracles. Expecting something to happen energizes your goal, and gives it momentum.

However, the expectations must be accompanied by actions consistent with materializing the expectations. It is not sufficient to merely wish something into existence, without pursuing accompanying relevant action.

Day 6 review

You have reflected for the past 5 days on different Inspirational Reflections in this book. You should now indicate what insights you got from your reading. List below at least 2 or 3 insights that you got from the Reflections, or information that was reinforced or confirmed.

_____

_____

_____

_____

Day 7 review

You have reflected for the past 6 days on different Inspirational Reflections. To get the best from the material, list below at least 2 areas or particular situations in your life in which you commit to do better.

_____

_____

_____

_____

171. Old habits are not easily changed

Your actions generate your success, or produce your disappointment. However, many of your actions are the results of your habits. You have unconsciously formed habits as you grew into adulthood.

Very often you merely say, "this is me, I cannot do differently." While coaching one of my clients—a very successful one—I pointed out that he had a powerful vision, but he needed to record in fair detail how he was going to shift from being a multi millionaire to the billionaire he wanted to be

My client's first response was that he always kept things in his head, and he did not need to introduce a new recording system. After some discussion he admitted that his old system did produce marvelous Results—he is a multi millionaire—but it had not taken him to his next higher level of being a billionaire. Old habits are not easily changed.. You do need to change some of your old habits that cannot deliver the new goal that you want.

Check your habits to determine if you can drop, or modify some of them to embrace the new targets you have. Do drop at least one habit that is not serving you well and in three months you will discover the positive difference it has made to the life you want. You need to become a new person to take you to anew level of achievement.

172. Your response to life

What happens to you and around you is insignificant, in relation to what lies within you. There are four things that are important to your life:

- your hereditary
- your environment
- your core values
- your response to your hereditary and environment.

You do not have any conscious opportunity in this world to determine your parents. Your hereditary flows from parenthood. Whether your parents are Chinese, African, Indian, Caucasian or some combination, you are who you are. Your hereditary is given and cannot be changed. Your response to your persona is key. Know that you are beautiful, you are worthy, and stand in your self-esteem.

Your environment impacts greatly on your life. You cannot change your environment to any great extent. You can be in it, but not of it. Of course there is the choice of leaving the particular environment. You will still be limited by your new environment. What needs to be done is to respond appropriately to what is happening to you, and around you. Your attitude to your environment is a solution. Maintain positive expectancy.

Let the core values you espouse guide you. While you cannot change your hereditary and environment, you have control over your reaction to them. Respond with creative insight and faith, and you will climb the highest mountain. The power of your mind can overcome any obstacle. Develop a strong desire for what you want. Pursue it resolutely, and take relevant massive action. Live your greatness.

173. Have singleness of purpose

An experience I had with a client showed the importance of being focused. She was concerned that commissions from her selling had dropped from TT$63,000 per month to TT$45,000. When we reviewed the situation it became clear that she was involved in too many things that were not connected to her main objective of generating tremendous monthly sales.

This reminded me of the tenet that your involvement in too many unconnected activities is the enemy of success. Decide what is your primary goal, and focus intensely on delivering it. Yes, review what is happening in your life. Are you pursuing urgent and secondary things, rather than primary and critical activities?

Focus is the name of the game. Your time is limited to 24 hours in a day. Your financial resources are limited, in that you do not have the money to do all the things you would like. Your energy is limited. Your emotions have breaking points. Thus, you need to be focused and intentional to deliver what you want in life. This is an excellent time to ponder whether you are focused enough to generate the happiness you desire. Be intentional!

174. Roadblocks to success

You came into this world at birth and you will surely die, as we all must. However, what is important is not your birth or death but how you lived between those two events.

You have to live your life fully and successfully. How can you do this? Acknowledge where you are, and what you have, and start now. Don't wait. Take one small step, and then another, and another. A journey starts with one small step. Think about it. How many ideas you have had, but they got nowhere. Start, take one step after another, and adjust as you go along to deliver the eventual result you want.

As you pursue your life's journey and pursue your dreams and goals, there are seven roadblocks to overcome. Be alert to which ones affect you and systematically overcome them:

- Lack of clarity and focus
- Insufficient desire
- Wrong or inadequate beliefs
- Limited knowledge
- Lack of skills and tools
- Poor health and fitness
- Inadequate support

Of these the two major stumbling blocks are:

- lack of clarity and focus
- insufficient desire.

If you are not clear on what you want, then there will be difficulty in achieving it. Clarity of intention, and focus are crucial for your success. It is the strength of your desire that gives you the impetus to overcome any difficulty or obstacle. Without great passion or desire you will give up pursuing your goal in the face of any threat, difficulty or obstacle. Success is dependent on belief in yourself, and the support of people around you who are committed to your success.

175. To be victorious you must believe in your cause

Think about something, then suggest to yourself that what you are thinking about is possible, and this lays the groundwork for a self-fulfilling prophecy. When you think that something is possible, you create the environment to make it happen. However, there is a bridge connecting your initial thoughts about something, and materializing those thoughts. That bridge is faith. Faith has been defined as being "the substance of things hoped for, the evidence of things not seen." To be victorious you must believe in your cause.

Faith empowers you to move forward although you cannot logically see a way forward. You must exercise mind sight and not eyesight. What you can see and what you can understand—eyesight—by its very nature cannot reveal the whole picture.

There is the unseen, and the undiscovered element the present state of knowledge cannot unmask. Think it's possible, walk by faith and not by sight, and you will conquer all obstacles in your path.

Day 6 review

You have reflected for the past 5 days on different Inspirational Reflections in this book. You should now indicate what insights you got from your reading. List below at least 2 or 3 insights that you got from the Reflections, or information that was reinforced or confirmed.

_____

_____

_____

_____

Day 7 review

You have reflected for the past 6 days on different Inspirational Reflections. To get the best from the material, list below at least 2 areas or particular situations in your life in which you commit to do better.

_____

_____

_____

_____

176. The challenges of relationships

There is a view that dependency causes compromise, and can result in resentment and internal splitting. To have harmonious relationships with those around you, early in life, you create false selves. You have different masks you put on. Thus, if the person you are dealing with does not like that mask, you can take it off. Your intrinsic self is still in tact. The mask protects you if you are rejected, to recover in the encounter. Your different masks protect your sense of self.

As you grow older you are trapped in past patterns, experience and assumptions that are invalid today. Your energy is directed, consciously or unconsciously, blaming others and circumstances for your frustrations. Take responsibility for your own life now, so you can consciously confront, forgive, and forget the past. This will provide your true independence. You will then be able to be interdependent with integrity, and without attachment or ulterior motives.

Without meaning of, and purpose for, your relationships you feel incomplete. Lack of purpose is one of the greatest causes of disease and depression today. You feel empty. You feel pain. In healing your relationships with the past, you heal yourself, and contribute to the healing of others. To get the best from relationships, you must develop and balance all major areas of your life. Polish your communication skills, deepen your spirituality, and use insights gained from your journey.

You need companionship for success. It does not have to be a sexual relationship. The dynamics of companionship satisfy the desire for you to be fulfilled as a human being. You need someone whom you can rely on, and trust. You need someone to listen, encourage, and support you in times of difficulty, distress, and success. You need someone to accept you as you are. Life will feel empty, if after your success there is no one to share the triumph. This is the challenge, and the reward of companionship.

177. Sweep your mind clean

You usually sweep your house clean for a festive season. In fact, you rid yourself of things that are not useful. You have spruced up around your home. This is at the external level. Good show!

You can do the same thing with your life. You can sweep your mind clean of all negative things. Examine the habits, values, practices and philosophy that are not serving your best interests. You can identify them, and commit to bringing more light and success to your future.

Examples of what might be frustrating your success are: postponing decisions, wasting valuable time, viewing too much television, abuse of cell phones, listening to unproductive radio, or excessive gossip. You can zero in on what is applicable to your situation.

Additionally, strengthen those things that have been producing good results in your life, or have the potential to release your greatness. Some of these are: powerful goals, reading motivational books, effectively managing your daily activities, holding your vision, being passionate about your purpose in life, and taking massive appropriate action to realize your million dollar dream desires. Reflect on what is happening in your life, and further your journey of significance.

178. Negative self-talk does not help you

Your thoughts operate at a subtle and powerful level, and govern your mind. and activities. Thoughts govern your desires, actions, and bodily movements.

However, the area that you spend most time with is your self-talk. You are continuously carrying on a conversation with yourself. You are assessing, analyzing and, among other things, being judgmental. In this process you tend to focus on negative aspects of your life such as:

- money you do not have.
- physical attributes that you are missing
- skills that you do not have
- your lack of influential friends

These negative thoughts you have of yourself are your worst enemies. They limit and dull your progress. You have the power over your own thoughts. Be responsible to yourself, and commit today to minimize your negative thoughts. Commit today to replace them with uplifting thoughts, and thoughts that create your better future.

179. Glimpse your brilliance

An interesting success principle is that you must have a great and burning desire to win. When there is this overriding commitment you do what it takes to succeed. You develop a focus that makes you unstoppable. This accounts in great part for Tiger's success as an international master of golf, breaking so many golfing records.

Your laser like focus will give you a glimpse of what is possible through sustained effort and concentration. This glimpse of what's possible occurs when you find something you love, and go after it without giving up.

We are all living below our potential. You can get a glimpse of what's possible if you dare to dream big, and risk without being reckless. You can be stronger, more confident and decisive, improve your self-image and interpersonal skills. In the process you will become happier and more self-fulfilled.

Do not let your poor self-esteem, self confidence and self image stop you from living your greatness. Examine your life today and take action for just one small improvement. It may be a trifle step, but while perfection is no trifle, trifles make perfection.

You have the power within you to make more money, establish new and better relationships, step up the spiritual ladder, and accomplish whatever you want.

It is your time now to design the life you want. Are you willing to step into your blessed and highly favored future? Claim your miracle. Take the first step. It does not have to be right or perfect. Then take the next step, and keep the momentum going. You can explode your potential, and live your greatness. Do this and you will rise to the top.

180. Learn from your errors, and move on

You are not perfect and therefore cannot succeed at everything you do. Let your definition of failure help, and not hinder you. One positive way of looking at failure is to consider that the only time you really fail is when you give up, or stop trying.

For example, Walt Disney was refused finance for his Disney World project by 302 banks before he got financed. Walt Disney would have only failed if he stopped trying to get the bank loan, and gave up going from bank to bank. When you accept the lessons of failure, and avoid repeating your errors you will be exploring your world, and moving on.

A fool learns from his own failures, while a wise man learns from the failures of others. It is therefore useful to examine the lives of great men and women—read their biographies and autobiographies—and learn from their mistakes.

Day 6 review

You have reflected for the past 5 days on different Inspirational Reflections in this book. You should now indicate what insights you got from your reading. List below at least 2 or 3 insights that you got from the Reflections, or information that was reinforced or confirmed.

_____

_____

_____

_____

Day 7 review

You have reflected for the past 6 days on different Inspirational Reflections. To get the best from the material, list below at least 2 areas or particular situations in your life in which you commit to do better.

_____

_____

_____

_____

Seize the moment

181. Accept yourself, and strive to make better decisions

You are unique. Your fingerprints are different from those of anyone else. Your blood composition is different to any other person. This suggests that you should accept yourself. You will not always be what you want to be. You may not always achieve what you have in mind. You may even fall short of your own values sometimes. But you are you. You have nothing to be ashamed about.

When you act, you do so because you think it is in your best personal interest—whether that be in your economic, spiritual, social, short term or long term interest. With hindsight you may have acted differently. At the time you acted, you took the best decision you could with the information then at your disposal. Thus, have no regrets, no apologies.

Use your experiences to make better decisions in the future. Accept yourself, change marginally where this is possible, and life will be a joy for you.

182. Do something different, if you want different results

Success has been defined as the progressive realization of worthwhile goals. You are standing at some point now in relation to the job you want, a relationship you wish to develop, a vacation you want to have in your favorite place, the development of your spiritual gifts, or simply more income to meet your needs. To get from where you are now to the particular goal you have in mind will require new success strategies and appropriate action.

Your goal is in the future, and you cannot see all the issues of the future clearly. This is a human condition. You cannot forecast accurately every event in the future that you require to accomplish your goals.

Even the path you take may be wrong. The importance of this is that you must not be discouraged when things go wrong.

Winston Churchill defined courage as going from failure to failure without losing enthusiasm. View your mistakes as a signal not to repeat that inappropriate action. When things are not working for you, do something different, keep persisting and success will be yours.

183. Get sufficient information before you move to the level of decision

Your mind is able to operate in creative ways, and to draw conclusions on the basis of insufficient evidence. You can make deductions and inferences from circumstantial evidence. This places a duty on you to believe things on the basis of solid evidence. This merely means that you need to get all the information and data before you move to the level of decision, or judgment.

Further, the information or evidence can be of differing quality, and you also need to know the nature of the evidence. For example, is the information hearsay, or has it been verified, or is there other corroborative evidence. The answers to the quality and nature of the information will determine how much reliance you can place on it. In turn you will know whether you can rely on the evidence to make a judgment, or whether the nature of the evidence compels you to suspend your judgment on the associated matter. Analyze and explore before you decide.

184. Great discoveries occur through visioning

Without vision the people perish. To survive you have to see things that are not there yet. To survive you have to anticipate correctly what the future holds. You have to imagine the possibilities, if you wish to move from one position to another. Since they are only possibilities, your ability to visualize and create mentally are crucial.

There is a view that you see through your eyes, and not with your eyes. Sight takes place in the mind, and the eyes are like the lens of the camera. The eyes physically record.

Any great discovery occurs through the ability to see things that, at first hand, do not appear to exist. It may be Columbus discovering that the world was not flat. It could be the great discovery of an antibiotic drug, or the discovery of the microchip. The idea may not yet have been crystallized, or the event materialized—they are still invisible. The art of seeing these invisible things is the exercise of vision, and this is necessary for your success. Do you have to see it before you can believe it, or do you have to believe it before you can see it? Ponder on this.

185. Learn to face and confront your fear

Fear grips every person in one-way, or another. You fear some possible event, or condition taking place. Fear is the phantom of the unknown. Can you conquer fear? To fight fear you must do the thing you fear most. If you fear the darkness, you have to arrange to go into the darkness. If you fear taking examinations, you have to simulate examination conditions, and write past papers under examination conditions.

Fear is a normal human response, so do not be afraid to face and confront your fear. The admonition "fear not" is given 365 times in the Bible. If you fear something and you postpone doing it, you simply increase your fear of it.

Fear is called the phantom of the unknown, because fear dwells in your imagination. Fear is a spirit. St. Paul expresses it well in 2.Timothy 1:7, "For God has not given us the spirit of fear, but of power and of love and of a sound mind."

If you want to conquer your fear, do what you fear three times. The first time is to prove that you can do it. The second time is to confirm that you can do it. The third time do it to see if you like doing it. After that you will be cleared of the particular fear.

Day 6 review

You have reflected for the past 5 days on different Inspirational Reflections in this book. You should now indicate what insights you got from your reading. List below at least 2 or 3 insights that you got from the Reflections, or information that was reinforced or confirmed.

_____

_____

_____

_____

Day 7 review

You have reflected for the past 6 days on different Inspirational Reflections. To get the best from the material, list below at least 2 areas or particular situations in your life in which you commit to do better.

_____

_____

_____

_____

CHAPTER 5: CHOOSE WISELY

186. Accept the consequences of your choices

The law of cause and effect states that what you sow you will reap. Anything that occurs is produced by a cause. It does not just happen by chance. Your thoughts are also largely responsible for the situations in which you find yourself.

Your thoughts have power. You become what you think. Very subtly and patiently, you act out your most secret thoughts. There are laws, traditions and practices that govern society. Within this framework you are free to choose what you want to do.

The power of personal choice is the birthright of every human being. But every choice brings with it some result, and you have to accept the consequences of your choice.

The nature and quality of your thoughts determine your choices and actions. You attract what you think. You create your life by the thoughts you cultivate. Your choices in the past have made you the person you are today. So have pure and good thoughts, and consistently choose wisely to become the future you want.

187. Appreciate what you have,

It is the nature of man to want more and more. This is a function of man's imperfection. You know that whatever condition you are in, the situation could be better. Your striving for perfection thus leads you to focus on what you do not have. It is thus easy for you to become concerned, and to go easily to the next step of complaining. What you lose sight of, is the abundance that you have, the blessings that you have, and the accomplishments that you have achieved.

One example will illustrate the point. You may be dissatisfied about the job that you have. You may want more money, you may believe that you merit a promotion, or perhaps you are just unhappy with your present job. There is nothing wrong with wanting to better yourself. You should certainly take appropriate action to achieve your new career goal.

However, you require balance in your life. Enjoy what you have got. Many persons do not even have a job. Be thankful for your present job while you aspire to something better. Take the action necessary to move you to your next point of achievement.

188. Smell the roses on life's journey

Life is for living. When your life force leaves your body you no longer function. As the Psalmist David said, " ... in the grave who shall give Thee thanks... " Reality is that by the sweat of your brow you eat bread. This places a special emphasis on the business in your life. That is, the manner in which you earn to provide for yourself, and family.

You may ask, what does living life mean for you? Life has three major components. First, an awareness of yourself, determining your purpose, what you want out of life, and setting your goals to meet your desires. The second component of life is following the appropriate strategies and taking the relevant action to accomplish your goals. The third component of living is to enjoy what you have achieved.

In life, most persons set their goals, and achieve at least 50% of them. However, few persons enjoy their achievements. Enjoy your achievements. Stop to smell the roses on life's journey.

189. Happiness is different from pleasure

Life is a gift you have which must be used wisely. You are made up of a physical body, a mental body and a spiritual body. Your physical side is the most obvious of your three bodies. This leads you quite often to concentrate on the physical or material things in your life. You thus focus on your creature comforts—the house, the car, the clothes, and the material things that other persons can provide for you. There is absolutely nothing wrong with wanting to get material things.

However, you ought to understand that they will not bring joy to you. Other people and material things can bring pleasure to you. They can give you pleasure, or withhold pleasure. On the other hand, happiness is an inside job. You determine, or you are responsible for, your own happiness. No one can provide or withhold your happiness.

Happiness produces the joy within your soul. Joy resides in you, and not in the things around you. You derive happiness from using your talents in the service of others. Cultivate a mindset of happiness.

190. Give, sow and contribute for your prosperity

The Universe has definite laws that govern it. One of those laws operates through the principle of a particular action being required to generate another specific result. If you want to get a benefit, you must first give a benefit. Another way of looking at this principle is to imagine that you have a bucket of water, and you pour some of that water to fill a glass. Until you empty or give up that glass of water, you cannot get the glass refilled from the source in the bucket.

Nature also gives a good example of the need for you to contribute before you can benefit. Food crops become available to be reaped, and so provide an important source of sustenance for the population. But before you can reap the harvest, you must sow the seed. The lesson to be learnt is that you need to give, to sow and to contribute, if you want to be truly prosperous. Sow seeds of kindness towards others, and sow multiple seeds of contribution, and you will become a person of value and success.

Day 6 review

You have reflected for the past 5 days on different Inspirational Reflections in this book. You should now indicate what insights you got from your reading. List below at least 2 or 3 insights that you got from the Reflections, or information that was reinforced or confirmed.

_____

_____

_____

_____

Day 7 review

You have reflected for the past 6 days on different Inspirational Reflections. To get the best from the material, list below at least 2 areas or particular situations in your life in which you commit to do better.

_____

_____

_____

191. Desires and core values are interrelated

As a baby you do not have the wisdom of the world, and you have to be nurtured by your parents or guardian. This guidance continues into your teenage years through your teachers, and then through your employers in the workplace. What this all means is that quite often you do not really know what you want. You have been continuously pointed to what you should be, or have.

You have not been allowed to develop your own thinking strategies to impact your life, as you want it to be. Thus, if you ask the next 10 persons you meet what they want out of life, you will notice generally their hesitancy to answer.

Today can be a new beginning in your life. Consider the options available to you, ponder on how these options fit into the core values you have adopted, and decide what you want out of life. When you determine this first essential step of what you want out of life, take appropriate action, and go after it with a lot of enthusiasm, and full commitment.

192. Imagination is integral to accomplishment

Seeing all that is within the realm of possibility, and seeing how it can be done, constitutes your imagination. Your imagination is your personal laboratory. Within your imagined world you can create events, map out plans, and visualize overcoming obstacles. Imagination is your first link to making the practical become possible.

The power to create the future lies in the imagination. Other than automatic reaction formed through habit, whatever you want to do you have first to think about it. Thus, if you imagine with great feeling, yourself accomplishing some particular feat, then you are likely to succeed in that feat.

The power of the imagination works for both positive and negative things. For example in the Bible Job cried out, " . . . the thing that I feared greatly has come upon me . . ." The lesson to be learned then is to give your imagination full reign to roam, and claim positive accomplishments in your life. If you can imagine it, you can with focus and persistence accomplish it.

193. Plan and plant your dreams

You may want to pick a mango from a tree in your yard from time to time. You can very simply go to one of the plant nurseries, buy a seedling and plant your julie mango tree. Some time later the tree will mature and juicy julie mangoes will be available to you. In the same way that you can plant a mango tree and get results, you can plant a dream that will come true.

You first have to know the dream precisely. In the case of the julie mango tree just discussed, you did not want a lime tree, or an avocado tree. The dream must be clear. What you focus on grows stronger in your life. If you keep a steadfast focus on your dream, the appropriate action necessary to materialize it will occur to you.

Be relentless in pursuing your dream for it to become a reality. Activate your power to be the best that you can be. Plant your dream. Nurture it, cultivate it, cherish it, and then you will fulfill it.

194. How to get to your next higher level

When you establish where you are at present, you can then decide whether you wish to remain there, or to go to another place. If you decide to move from where you are, you can then judge better what to do to get there, and how to do it. An example will make this clear. If you determine that you are in Port of Spain, and you wish to go to San Fernando, you know that what you have to do is travel to San Fernando. But how will you do it? There are several choices. You may walk, run, take public transport, use your own or a friend's vehicle, go by sea or air.

What is crucial is to know where you are, where you want to go, what to do to get there, and how to do it. Pursue your goals rigorously, and you will live a full and meaningful life.

195. Accomplish your goals daily and experience it's joy

Understand the human spirit by observing how a young baby operates. While a baby is still at the creeping stage notice how he/she investigates the surroundings. No one has instructed the baby. On its own, the human spirit of the baby is looking to accomplish, to achieve, or to triumph. It is the nature of the human being to give expression to its creativity and potential, through doing things.

Deny the human spirit this essence and you will destroy its happiness.

One view is that human beings are aware of their imperfections, and they seek to do things better. When they triumph, happiness occurs. What cannot be denied is that anyone who accomplishes, triumphs or achieves experiences feelings of joy and happiness. So set about accomplishing your goals on a daily basis and you will travel the road of happiness.

Day 6 review

You have reflected for the past 5 days on different Inspirational Reflections in this book. You should now indicate what insights you got from your reading. List below at least 2 or 3 insights that you got from the Reflections, or information that was reinforced or confirmed.

_____

_____

_____

_____

Day 7 review

You have reflected for the past 6 days on different Inspirational Reflections. To get the best from the material, list below at least 2 areas or particular situations in your life in which you commit to do better.

_____

_____

_____

196. Emphasize right things in life to get right results

If you wish to bring about a particular set of right results in your life, this is achieved by making the right efforts. You may put tremendous effort into what you do, but if it is not the correct effort, the results you hope for will not occur.

Put the emphasis on the right things and live the life you believe to be right. If you then do not achieve what you hoped for, you will be able fully to overcome your disappointment. Your life should be so well balanced and centered, that any mishap in your life should not throw you off your center for a prolonged period.

No matter what misfortune overtakes you, there will still be a whole magnificent man or woman left, after being temporarily stripped of your hope. The essence of greatness is to know that virtue is enough. Be joyous, and let the spirit of peace be present when you journey.

197. Use picture words for powerful communication

When someone speaks to you or if you are reflecting, you think in pictures and not in words. You associate images with the words you hear, or think about. When you hear the word circus, what comes to your mind? Clowns, or elephants, or other circus events that have impressed you may come to your mind. The point is that you did not think the letters "c i r c u s." Your thoughts were in pictures, not in words.

This attribute of the human mind can be used to support what you want to achieve in life. First, at the level of communicating with others, you should consciously use picture words that will help your listeners to get your message better. These picture words are sometimes called emotional words. The public orator, whether he be politician, priest or motivational speaker, use this fact to great advantage to get their message across.

Second, you can place in your home or work place actual pictures—a house, a car, or a relationship—of whatever you want to achieve. Place the pictures in key places, such as your bathroom mirror, or wallet, so you get success reinforcement continually. Work with picture words and actual pictures to strengthen your success patterns.

198. What is the life you really want?

You go through every day reflecting on the life that you think will bring you peace, happiness, and fulfillment. It is a fact that thoughts are the father of action. Actions produce habits, and this in turn creates the life you experience.

Thus, you should examine what is happening to you in these areas to keep on course to get your heart's desires. The first requirement is that you should have written in clear and specific terms what it is that you want for your life. Congratulations if you have already documented your plan of direction. Visit the document and confirm that you have not changed your mind. If you have not met this first requirement, get going, and do it.

Next, examine what are the two or three strategies that you have to commit to, so that you will be on your way to success. For example, you may need to spend less time being aimless, and doing unrewarding things. Accompanying your strategies should be definite action plans to deliver your intentions. If you are going on vacation, you spend some time planning it. Your life needs planning also.

An interesting point is if your actions produce habits that do not serve delivery of what you want in life. If so, then re-assess your actions, and build new capacity consistent with your goals.

You have the power to create the future you want. The choice is yours to design the future you want, but this has to be with a commitment to dedicated action that is consistent, relevant, and focused. You are the star of your show. Produce it.

199. Inspire others to blossom

You are a beacon of light, but you are not always aware that you are shining light in the darkness of another's life. You have unique talents, and other persons often watch your life closely and silently. Thus, you have the ability to affect the lives of others through your normal behavior. Be alive, awake, and alert to your awesome responsibility.

The lesson you must learn is that every day of life should be filled with enlightening words and action that will help to expand you, and develop you into someone more valuable to yourself, and to others.

The greatest gift you can give others is your caring, connection and gentle guidance. You might not be aware that you are a role model for the people in your life. Your every action is being watched. Someone is looking to you for inspiration, support and leadership

Thus, be conscious of your every thought, word, and action to manifest the best that you can be, and consequently positively impact and inspire the people around you. Connect with your environment.

An old proverb says, "One who refreshes others, will himself be refreshed." So, be an inspiration for someone, and blossom into the fullness of your greatness.

200. If your mind tells you can, then you can

When you think of doing something, your belief of whether you can do it is important. When you believe you can do something, half the battle is won. The mind is a powerful instrument. The mind sets the limits to what you can do. It overrides your potential. If in fact you can do something, but your mind says to you that you cannot do it, then the reality is you will not be able to do it.

Each person has a special ability to look at a situation, and to know whether it is possible to deal with that situation. The complicating factor is that you may lack self-confidence with respect to that particular matter. You have to believe in yourself. You have to reach deep within your soul, and feel that you can do the job at hand. Then, through your thoughts and actions create the world that you want.

Belief governs every situation in your life. One aspect is the inner feeling that you can accomplish whatever you undertake. With positive and creative thinking your opportunities can be grasped and materialized. Believe in the potential of yourself.

Day 6 review

You have reflected for the past 5 days on different Inspirational Reflections in this book. You should now indicate what insights you got from your reading. List below at least 2 or 3 insights that you got from the Reflections, or information that was reinforced or confirmed.

_____

_____

_____

_____

Day 7 review

You have reflected for the past 6 days on different Inspirational Reflections. To get the best from the material, list below at least 2 areas or particular situations in your life in which you commit to do better.

_____

_____

_____

201. Increase your knowledge for greater success

The world has entered the learning revolution. That means that you must increase your knowledge on a continuing basis. Change is taking place at a faster rate than in previous times. Technology is advancing at a rapid pace. Be part of the global movement of change, and increasing knowledge.

Establish a goal to be powerful, proud, strong and self-confident. Read books and other material, listen to audios, view DVDs, and have intelligent discussions. Understand that knowledge makes the world go around. Consider the adage, "He who knows not, and knows that he knows not is a wise man, cultivate him." Also, he who knows not, and does not know that he knows not, deceives himself, shun him.

Be conscious of the great strides that are taking place in knowledge daily. Resolve to close your knowledge gap by gathering information daily in a consistent, structured manner.

202. Engage in worthwhile activity for your success

You either grow or decay. You do not remain unchanged. Activity is the means by which change takes place. Activity is the oil that keeps the wheel of life from becoming rusty and jammed. Nature gives you the clue of the importance of activity. The earth revolves around the sun to get its sustenance from the rays of the sun. The tides of the sea ebb and flow continuously to preserve its functions.

Human beings operate on the physical, emotional, psychological and spiritual levels. Activity is demonstrated on the physical level quite easily. This occurs when you build something, write something, teach others, or support nature through growing vegetables, fruits and flowers.

The emotional and psychological areas are subtle. You draw inferences of their operation from other evidence in your life. For example, when you are in a depressed state, or when your present reaction is triggered because of a similar event in the past.

The spiritual level is quite interesting. You cannot ordinarily see your spirit. Some people refer to this as the life force. What is certain is that when this life force leaves your body and does not return, death occurs. You can pump any amount of oxygen and food into that physical body, but it will not respond, if the life force has left it.

Another concept is that at the spiritual level you maneuver your life to accomplish what you want. The concept posits that you are a spiritual being having a physical experience, and not the other way around.

How can you experience an inner feeling of joy, accomplishment and happiness? If you want to be really happy, avoid being idle, and use your talents in a worthwhile activity that inspires you, and uplifts your environment.

203. Actions produce your banquet of consequences

What you sow, you reap. When events occur in your life, you can link them to actions you have taken, or failed to have taken in the past, Each action you take has consequences. Things and events do not just happen in your life. They are caused. More importantly, they are caused by your own action, or lack of action.

The consequences might not occur immediately or when they do occur you may not relate your current situation to be a consequence of your previous action. For example, to be the best in your field requires rigorous and dedicated training. Your success is related to that previous dedicated set of actions in pursuit of your excellence.

Your health is another classic example. When in later life you suffer with diabetes, high blood pressure, arthritis or some other ailment, this is the consequence of your earlier previous life style, and eating habits. Good actions produce good consequences.

Your challenge then is always to let your actions be life supporting to yourself, your family and your environment. In this way, you will create a banquet of consequences that gives you a life of joy, peace, prosperity and happiness.

204. Your innermost beliefs will take you over troubled waters

What gives you character is your philosophy. Consider all the things you have heard in your lifetime: all the things you know and believe, then pick out what are the most important things for you, and that is your philosophy.

Your life is governed by the core values you hold dear to you. Things will be happening all around you, and to you. Your response or reaction to the events occurring will depend on your internal point of reference. Your innermost beliefs will take you over troubled waters.

Your faith will keep you centered when conditions are difficult. Core values of persistence and relentlessness will give you the drive to accomplish, and the strength to withstand grave difficulties. Review your core values, and commit to observing them rigorously.

205. Compromise and tolerance support your success

You are different to everyone else, but not so different that you cannot get along with others. You are interdependent. This requires you to be at peace with yourself, and then to be at peace with others. Any issue can be seen from several points of view.

If you look at a large elephant, depending on your position, the trunk and front legs may be visible. A person in another position may only see the elephant's tail and back legs. The bigger and more complex the issue, the more likely it is that you will have a different view to another person.

The challenge is to try to understand the different views of others, and to visualize the bigger picture. With the spirit of patience, compromise and tolerance you can converse, work out your differences with others, and arrive at a solution that benefits all the parties. Work on understanding others, rather than on insisting that others must first understand you.

Day 6 review

You have reflected for the past 5 days on different Inspirational Reflections in this book. You should now indicate what insights you got from your reading. List below at least 2 or 3 insights that you got from the Reflections, or information that was reinforced or confirmed.

_____

_____

_____

_____

Day 7 review

You have reflected for the past 6 days on different Inspirational Reflections. To get the best from the material, list below at least 2 areas or particular situations in your life in which you commit to do better.

_____

_____

_____

_____

CHAPTER 6: BE EMPOWERED AND RELEASE YOUR BRILLIANCE

206. Successful people do not quit because of their mistakes

All success requires action. But the action must be relevant and appropriate to what you want to achieve. This calls for a structured approach for reaching your goals. You need to have a plan.

The first part of the plan merely says that you are here now, and you want to get to another point over there. How to get from here to there, in broad terms, constitutes the plan.

The success model is then plan, act, review; then adjust the plan, act, review, and carry this process on and on. That is how successful people keep on the move. The plan is about the future that is uncertain. No one has all the knowledge so the strategies sometimes fail.

Mistakes occur, but successful people do not quit because of mistakes. They learn lessons from their mistakes and don't repeat them. Be relentless, use the review of your plan to keep on track, and success will be yours.

207. Are you modeling or living aimlessly?

Human beings tend to copy what they see happening around them. Consider how a baby grows. The baby adopts the patterns that are visible around him/her. It starts with walking, talking and emotional responses of those around.

In adulthood, you have the choice of being a model yourself, following a model, or simply just existing aimlessly. When you find your purpose and you relentlessly pursue it, you attract attention of others.

Your path has its difficulties, and as you overcome them, you provide the possibility for someone else to follow in your footsteps. You have shown the way of success in spite of the valleys of despair. If your journey is seen as having integrity, this can led to your becoming a model for others. The formula for becoming a model is being on purpose, pursuing your goals relentlessly, and with honor, justice and integrity.

Quite often, before you can become a model, you have to follow a model yourself. You have to learn the basics. How can you learn, unless you have a teacher? The worst possible option is to be neither a model, nor follow a model, but exist aimlessly. You can be yourself a model, follow a model or simply exist aimlessly. The choice is yours.

208. Character Traits of Successful People

When you examine the lives of successful people, there are certain common traits as follows:

- Delivering more than expected
- Persevere
- Honest
- Solution oriented
- Friendly
- Life long learners
- Hardworking

They deliver more than is expected, and thus become persons of value to others. They follow the principle of under-promising, and over-delivering.

They keep on going despite difficulties and disappointments. Others give up just when success is around the corner. Successful people continue although they cannot see the light at the end of the tunnel.

They maintain honesty in dealing with others. They do not deceive to get a short-term advantage. They are fair, reliable, and transparent.

They are solution oriented. They see problems as opportunities to move forward, and effect solutions.

They are friendly. They relate well with others, and this enables them to lead others to accomplish the task.

They are life long learners. They understand that change and innovation are taking place rapidly, and so they keep abreast of new knowledge in their fields and associated areas.

They are hard working in the sense that they are persistent and consistent in their tasks. Moreover they work hard, but smart as well. They ensure that what is being done is as simple and best as it can be done.

Consequently, if you want to be successful, cultivate the above traits, and deepen them where they already exist.

209. Dialogue your ideas to be successful

Your life is governed by developing and refining ideas that you have. If you merely keep ideas to yourself, this will not serve your personal development. Your success occurs when you take your vision, views, values, concerns, and formulate them in such a manner that you get the support necessary to accomplish your goals. This comes through an exchange of ideas with others.

You have to move from your own monologue to dialogue with persons within your area of activity. If you keep your thoughts to yourself without discussing it with someone, your fine ideas remain isolated and under-developed.

The acronym FEAR may stand for False Evidence Appearing Real. Fear is so crippling that it stops you from living to your fullest potential. In fact, to achieve your life's design, you must move beyond your fears.

You have very powerful thoughts, but you are afraid to speak them out for these reasons:

- You might be challenged
- You cannot justify your position
- You may believe that persons you admire or care for, will see you in an unfavorable light because of your views
- You don't have confidence in yourself
- You think you may appear foolish
- You fear that while speaking you will hear your own weakness

But you can change all of that.

One approach is to be clear that there are many different views about any one point. Quite often it is not a matter of being right or wrong.

The circumstances and the situation may demand appropriateness rather than infallibility.

With this insight you are free to express yourself without fearing disapproval. This will release you from the pressure of having to be right in your communications. You must still be logical, and have integrity in your dialogue, but you will be free from the fear of being wrong.

210. Monologue and dialogue - Part I

The greater your intellect, the more prone you are to indulge in monologue. This has been a great drawback for many such persons, as their great ideas, and creative genius remain stifled in their minds. Their thoughts keep going around and around in their heads, so no birth is given to great contributions they could make.

By its nature monologue jumbles your thoughts, and the deeper and complex the thoughts, the more likely that you will not be able to separate the elements in a holistic and structured way. Do not let this be your downfall. Find someone whom you can trust to enter into dialogue, so that your wonderful thoughts can crystallize into creative expression, and not remain as just insights

A key to your success is that you must be thinking in a deliberate manner for most of your day, and not be proceeding on automatic pilot for prolonged periods. Without automatic responses life would be impossible. Some examples are putting on your shoes, having a shower, and driving your car. However, your power to perform rests on the deliberate actions you take from moment to moment.

Day 6 review

You have reflected for the past 5 days on different Inspirational Reflections in this book. You should now indicate what insights you got from your reading. List below at least 2 or 3 insights that you got from the Reflections, or information that was reinforced or confirmed.

_____

_____

_____

_____

Day 7 review

You have reflected for the past 6 days on different Inspirational Reflections. To get the best from the material, list below at least 2 areas or particular situations in your life in which you commit to do better.

_____

_____

_____

_____

Proper preparation ensures success

211. Monologue and dialogue - Part II

The aim of dialogue is to:

- Enrich the pool of information
- Uncover the truth
- Explore the subject
- Improve existing positions
- Synthesize several points of view
- Exchange ideas

While you are in the process of speaking and developing your points, you get new insights and a deeper understanding of points that you are making. The purpose of the dialogue is to expose different points of view and so enrich the pool of information from which wiser decisions and actions can take place. Despite all of our technological wonders, a powerful tool of personal growth is something as simple as talking to each other

To be useful, dialogue must not descend to mere argument. For any particular issue there is a myriad of views. The truth of the matter may not reside exclusively in one of those views. Arguing who is right and who is wrong is really not productive.

Dialogue supports you to get what you want in life as your circle of family and friends can hold you accountable for whom you say you are. Moreover, they can support you to live the life of your dreams. Dare to step into powerful dialogue: it enriches your relationships.

212. Ask good questions – Part I

To be successful you have to think. Moreover, the quality of your thinking will determine your future. As you think, you invariably come up with questions for which you require answers. The questions normally start with the words who, why, when, what, and where. Questions arc useful since within the seed of the question resides the answer.

You cannot achieve your vision and your goals unless you ask discerning questions. A discerning question is one that goes to the root of the issue, and thereby draws out the elements that are necessary to discover the truth, or unravel the reality, by exploring differing views.

If you have any matter to resolve, simply ask the questions, and you will draw out useful information. These questions will trigger other questions, and bring out critical information that will give added insight to the issue.

However, you must be careful to frame the question in such a manner to support positive growth in your life. This requires you to make better choices of the questions you ask. Frame your questions well.

213. Ask good questions – Part II

Generally, your first reaction to situations is a negative one. This results from our training which focuses on what is not working, or on what is not right. You look for the exception. You concentrate on the variance, on what is missing, and not on what is present and good. This means that very often your first questions will be negatively directed. You must thus consciously ask a second and third question to get your perspective right with an appropriate positive question. Better questions lead to better results.

These simple guidelines create better questions:

- Let your question begin with "what" or "how" instead of "why" "when" or "who"
- The question should be personal and so contain the word "I" rather than "they" "them" "we" or "you"
- Provide an action step, or be action focused in your question.

These guidelines are intended to make you responsible for what is happening in your life. The "what" or "how" turns your attention inwards when combined with "I." The focus on action as opposed to grumbling or making excuses complete the excellent question. Putting it all together the question becomes " what can I do?"

214. Meaning of success – Part I

Success is being whom you want to be, and getting what you want. Looked at another way, success is the progressive realization of your worthwhile goals. What you aspire to achieve covers your material wants, and your spiritual fulfillment. One Sage makes the point that your need for happiness drives your whole life. Happiness is a spiritual construct. Man is body, soul and spirit so that to achieve success you have to satisfy not only bodily needs and your five senses, but also the spiritual part of your being.

It does not matter which religion you belong to, you have the Divine spark of the Creator within you. There are different administrations of the Spirit, but this Divine spirit is available to all through the majesty of the Creator.

Thus, there are spiritual laws that apply no matter your belief system. Just as the sun shines on the just and the unjust, no matter how they feel about the sun. Similarly, spiritual laws apply without being a respecter of persons.

215. Meaning of success – Part II

Manifesting your love is probably the most important and powerful tool in your quest for spiritual growth. Love God and love your neighbor as yourself sums up the spiritual equation. How to love when someone hurts you is not easy, but forgiveness is a key to your spiritual achievement. You also have to be big enough to accept the forgiveness of others whom you have hurt.

The success that you see in your life is merely the eyes with which you see your world. If you want an improved life you have to see yourself, and the way in which the world occurs for you, in a different manner. You have to see things differently, and do things differently to reach the pinnacle of your success.

Are you paying sufficient attention to your spiritual growth? Most times people identify being religious as being spiritual, but this is not necessarily the same thing. The height of spirituality is raising your consciousness and actions to the level of true fellowship with man and God. This means total obedience to His statutes and conformity with His perfect will.

Day 6 review

You have reflected for the past 5 days on different Inspirational Reflections in this book. You should now indicate what insights you got from your reading. List below at least 2 or 3 insights that you got from the Reflections, or information that was reinforced or confirmed.

_____

_____

_____

_____

Day 7 review

You have reflected for the past 6 days on different Inspirational Reflections. To get the best from the material, list below at least 2 areas or particular situations in your life in which you commit to do better.

_____

_____

_____

216. Stagnancy or transformation?

Do you want to remain where you are now spiritually, or do you want more spiritual enlightenment? It is the nature of the human being to reach for perfection, so you will automatically want to do better spiritually. However, you need to have the desire strongly enough to make your spiritual growth a reality.

The body is an outward expression of the spirit. What this means is that whatever your present circumstances are in the outer world is a reflection of what is going on in your inner world. That is, what is going on with you spiritually. This is an interesting notion.

What is happening to you now, for better or for worse, is the result of what kind of spiritual life you have been leading in the past. Do not let outward appearances fool you. It is the heart that matters. You may see someone's outward actions and be totally convinced that the person is a bad egg. You are not the judge. Look to the development of your own perfection. Every person will have to account for himself/herself. How then can you claim your Higher Self? There are many approaches, although there is only One Way—the Way of Truth, Light and Love.

Consider these four approaches or pathways to facilitate your spiritual growth. They are as follows:

- Communicating more often and more deeply with the Creator.
- Increasing your knowledge about spiritual things through regular reading of the Holy Scriptures, and not forsaking the Assembly.
- Strengthening your spiritual capabilities by practicing self-denial through guided fasting.
- Displaying a sense of gratitude through giving back some of your blessings to the Supreme Giver, through benefiting persons and benevolent organizations in need.
- Having an attitude of gratitude
- Learning to forgive those who hurt you

217. Become more of a spiritual adept

You already possess the values that can make you a spiritual giant. You know intuitively what is morally right and morally wrong. You are designed to resonate inwardly to know from the stirring of your heart the truth of any matter. It is only that your ego gets in the way and distorts the picture. You need to reflect more, and listen more intently to your inner voice.

Whatever you have as your spiritual life values, you are not being 100% faithful to them. For example, you know that you should always speak the truth; you know that you should be more prayerful; you know that you should read the word of God more often; you know that you should display gratitude by tithes, alms and thanksgiving. However, you are not observing these and other of your own values as fully as you could. Raise your standards to nearer 100% of what you know should be your guiding principles, and you will notice changes for the better in your life.

You will trigger an improvement in your link with God, an improvement in the quality of your relationships with others, and an improvement in the difficult circumstances of your life.

Follow these guidelines, and you will develop and strengthen your inner peace that is a critical element of spiritual progress, and the foundation for your success:

- Proceed intuitively, and be not fearful because of past bad experiences
- Enjoy each moment as it unfolds
- Refuse to judge other people
- Do not be concerned about interpreting the actions of others
- Lose interest in conflict
- Stop worrying needlessly
- Identify and appreciate your blessings
- Accept your connections to others and nature
- Practice smiling
- Accept your situation, but use wisdom to make it better
- Love yourself, and extend that love to others, and to the Divine
- Learn to accept the love given to you by others

218. Transform yourself for success – Part I

Do you require a breakthrough in your life? A personal breakthrough requires your personal commitment. Commitment is doing the thing you said you would do, long after your original positive mood or feelings have passed.

There are five pillars of commitment that provide the foundation for your personal transformation:

- Commit to knowledge enthusiastically
- Have an amazing commitment to your dreams
- Be a ferocious commitment to step outside your comfort zone
- Display a passionate commitment to love
- Persevere with an unstoppable attitude

219. Transform yourself for success – Part II

Personal transformation requires you to conform to the following requirements:

- You must have the passionate desire to improve the results in some specific area of your life.
- You must be willing to change or modify some actions you have taken in the past in the specific area you wish to change.
- You must be willing to be coached. It is difficult to learn unless you have a teacher/coach.
- You must resolve to be an invincible commitment to succeed at whatever you do.

Check the five main areas of your life and consider whether you wish to change habits in any of these areas that are not producing the results, or success you wish. The five areas are (i) career and finance,

(ii) relationships, (iii)religious or spiritual,(iv) health and exercise, and (v)personal development and recreation.

Your challenge is to come out of your comfort zone. You have to do things that are new, things that are unknown, and things that require you to take risks that you have not taken before. Personal transformation requires a shift in your awareness that you have the power to create the life you want.

Personal transformation is a journey that never ends. You continuously strive to be better and better at whatever you do. As your consciousness shifts, your desires and intentions shift. Be awake, aware, alive, and alert and you will, inch by inch, achieve your personal transformation.

220. Re-engineering for more success – Part I

Are you satisfied with your level of success? You are certainly putting in a great deal of time and effort, but things do not seem to be working, as you would like. If you are giving so much effort to what you do in life, why is it not coming together as you expect?

One answer is that your focus may be wrong, or not structured for success. That is, you may be placing your attention and efforts on the unimportant issues.

Following the Pareto Principle, otherwise known as the 80/20 Rule, can make you work more effectively and productively. This Rule states that 80% of your results are produced by 20% of your activities and efforts. Expressed another way, 20% of your results are produced by 80% of your activities and efforts.

From a people standpoint, the Pareto Principle shows that 80% of your satisfaction and enjoyment, comes from 20% of the people you spend your time with. The obverse of this is that you get only 20% of satisfaction and enjoyment from 80% of the people with whom you interact.

The 80/20 Rule is telling you that both in terms of your daily activities, and the people with whom you interact; only a small 20% is responsible for your results and interpersonal satisfaction

Do you get up early, go to bed late, work weekends and stress out yourself? Why are you spending so much of your time, money, effort, energy and resources doing things that have such a small payoff or reward? You have not consciously, and with focus examined what you are doing on a consistent basis. Review your activities. Put more attention on the 20% of activities that produce 80% of your results.

Day 6 review

You have reflected for the past 5 days on different Inspirational Reflections in this book. You should now indicate what insights you got from your reading. List below at least 2 or 3 insights that you got from the Reflections, or information that was reinforced or confirmed.

_____

_____

_____

_____

Day 7 review

You have reflected for the past 6 days on different Inspirational Reflections. To get the best from the material, list below at least 2 areas or particular situations in your life in which you commit to do better.

_____

_____

_____

_____

221. Re-engineering for more success – Part II

Your life is governed by training, habit, and tradition. Consider these areas and adjust your activities to optimize your potential.

When you were born you started with a clean slate. You start your training from babyhood, although some would say that your emotions and attitude start being formed in your mother's womb. It is said that a mother's condition during pregnancy affects the persona of the baby. Hence, babies' whose mothers were alcoholics or drug users pass on these tendencies to the babies.

Training or your formation is established within 7 to 8 years of birth. You learn to talk, walk, eat, and do a number of other things by example and instruction.

Thus, if you want to have a different lifestyle, or if you want different results in your life, you have to re-train or re-engineer yourself in critical aspects of what you think, do, and speak. For instance, if you live a life of fear, or of negative thinking, or a life of believing that good and great things will not happen to you, it will be necessary to get out of that mode.

You will need to be trained in faith, positive thinking, and thinking big. You will need to be trained to raise your self-esteem and self-confidence, recognize your great potential, and understand that a new grand life is possible for you to achieve.

222. Re-engineering for more success – Part III

Habits can control your destiny, if you do not for significant periods live your life consciously. A habit is an acquired behavior pattern regularly followed until it has become automatic. For example, brushing your teeth, smoking cigarettes, locking your car, and turning off the stove.

Habit is so ingrained, that you may not remember if you locked your car, or turned off the stove. Without habit life would be unbearable. Just think how often you drive your car without thinking of driving it.

The point of the illustrations is that if you want to change your life for the better, you have to change some of your habits that frustrate your desires. Consciously examine your habits. Eliminate those that are not working in your best interests. Add new habits that will support the new you that you desire.

223. Re-engineering for more success – Part IV

Tradition is how you do things based on what historically has been done in your family, or community environment. The true story is told of a newly married woman who was asked by her husband why she cut off the ends of the roast, before putting the roast in the oven to be baked. She said that her mother did it and so she has followed.

The husband asked the wife's mother who was visiting, the same question, and she said it was a family tradition, as her mother also cut off the ends of the roast before putting it in the oven.

Thereupon, the wife telephoned her grandmother to get the explanation. The grandmother said quite calmly that her oven was not big enough, so she had to cut off the ends of the roast so that it could fit in the oven.

What passes for tradition may be irrelevant for today's situation. Check on your traditions, and ensure that they are sensible and applicable to your life today.

224. Better personal connections generate success - Part I

You are shaped largely by the way in which people react to you. Your primary indication of who you are while at a young age, is the manner in which people respond to you, and treat you. If people treat you with kindness, respect, and courtesy, you are likely to believe that you merit such proper treatment.

Three basic social needs of humans that have been identified by Psychologists are affection, inclusion, and control. You have an ingrained desire for affection. You need to know that someone cares for you. The research shows that babies need to be stroked, and touched for their well-being and development.

One view holds that the connection between mother and child during pregnancy is the root of the need for affection. When the child is born, the long period of intimate physical connectivity is suddenly broken—the umbilical cord is severed at birth—and the previous intimacy between mother and child becomes a new need for the child.

As a baby, you are dependent on others for food, care and physical comfort, and this develops a dependency that eventually translates as a need for affection. The affection you require is not necessarily sexual. It is a call for a display towards you of genuine care, concern, and conviviality.

Affection is important for your emotional survival. Without it your life tends to echo emptiness. If you don't get affection you will develop harshness, suppressed anger, and an indifference to life. Thus, you should display genuine care and concern for others, and thereby attract similar energies in your life.

225. Better personal connections generate success - Part II

The need for inclusion is part of the process of your formation. From very young there is the natural desire to be part of some group. Reflect on your childhood. You felt most comfortable when you were with your immediate family, or children with whom you could relate and play. The manner in which society is organized also re-enforces the need for inclusion.

Your initial schooling quickly identifies groupings, and the need to belong to the group. This need is recognized and satisfied through various types of teams, houses, and specialized groups in schools.

Peer pressure is exercised to get persons to conform to the values of the group. A client explained to me how while he did not use drugs, his peer group did. In order to remain part of the group, he accompanied them to the drug dens when the group members were going to buy their quota of drugs. He really needed to be included in the group, so he was prepared to risk possible police confrontation.

Therefore, you need to be strong and have the courage of your values, and your convictions. Despite your need for inclusion, you have to stand for something. If you do not stand for something, you will fall for anything. Be strong and faithful to your core values, to avoid being led astray.

Day 6 review

You have reflected for the past 5 days on different Inspirational Reflections in this book. You should now indicate what insights you got from your reading. List below at least 2 or 3 insights that you got from the Reflections, or information that was reinforced or confirmed.

_____

_____

_____

_____

Day 7 review

You have reflected for the past 6 days on different Inspirational Reflections. To get the best from the material, list below at least 2 areas or particular situations in your life in which you commit to do better.

_____

_____

_____

_____

226. Better personal connections generate success - Part III

The desire for your being in control is related to the need you have to lead the life that you want. Some Psychologists believe that the basis for a positive mental attitude is a sense of control. Most stress is caused by being out of control of some critical part of your life that you consider important.

The need for control is often taken further. Attempts are made to control others. The underlying problem in relationships is that you want your views to prevail over those of other persons. When you do not get your way, the relationship breaks down. A matured relationship admits of dialogue and accommodating different views, since no one knows everything.

There is one view that the objective of karate is not to be victorious, but to perfect the character of its participants. Likewise, it is the ultimate aim of life that you should become everything you are capable of becoming. This becomes possible with the lessons that you learn through relationships with people, particularly those who are dear to you, or who are regularly in contact with you.

Relationships can be complex and complicated, so to build quality relationships, it is important to praise others, and let them know you appreciate their efforts. Do not complain, criticize, or condemn anyone, especially not even in your mind. Find opportunities to praise—genuine praise—persons with whom you are in contact.

227. Forms of intelligence

The outcome of relationships is strongly dependent on the knowledge, awareness, and consciousness of the participants. Individuals possess several different forms of intelligence. Two of these forms are inter-personal intelligence and intra-personal intelligence.

Inter-personal intelligence is your ability to relate with others. It is how well you communicate, persuade, negotiate, influence, and interact with others. You can upgrade your competence in this area of inter-personal intelligence through coaching and training.

Forming and maintaining good relationships is vital to success in both your personal life, and your career. Intra-personal Intelligence defines how well you get along with yourself. How well do you know yourself? Are you clear on the values for which you stand? Do you know both your strengths and weaknesses? Are you clear on your dreams and goals?

In short, you should know yourself, understand yourself, and thus be honest and objective with yourself, resulting in your being more honest and objective with others.

Factually, intra-personal intelligence is the bedrock upon which inter-personal intelligence is founded. You need to know yourself well before you can understand others to relate with them solidly.

228. Angles of personal development – Part I

You are different to any other individual. Over time your individual needs also differ. It is thus useful to examine different strategic development approaches.

First strategy: You have to change the picture of yourself if you wish to change your situation. If you want to do better in life, you have to be become better yourself. An element of change is to see yourself in that new condition of change—visualization.

Second strategy: This requires you to pursue these four concepts aggressively:

- Raise the performance level of your standards
- Change your limiting beliefs
- Develop new strategies for success
- Take massive action

Third strategy: You need to have a larger vision of yourself by observing the following five points:

- See yourself beyond your present circumstances.
- Decrease the amount of negative thoughts you have of yourself.
- Increase your self-worthiness.
- Invest in your continuing education.
- Bolster your strengths and minimize your weaknesses.

Fourth strategy: To be successful requires you to be Alive, Alert, and Awake. To benefit from being alive, you have to be aware of yourself and your surroundings. Being alive and awake, demands that you be alert to accomplish success. You must know what is happening in your environment, and be alert to the opportunities, and possibilities that are open to you. This will give you the power to be your fullest potential.

229. Angles of personal development – Part II

Consider the changes that you want to make in your life. Wherever you are situated now, you wish for something different. These elements of wanting more and striving for perfection, locate you in the labyrinth of change.

If you want to achieve something different from that which is occurring in your life now, there are three angles to consider:

- You have to change your thinking.
- You must make a series of new decisions
- You must take continuous new action in alignment with those new decisions

Change your actions, if you want a different result from that which you are getting at present. You must set challenging goals that stretch and excite you. You have to use your imagination despite the difficulties, negativity, and roadblocks that confront you.

Look at old issues with new and different insights. You have to see things differently, and do things differently to improve your life. You decided you wanted to change. Honor your commitment to change, and it will be done. Be focused on the changes you want in your life during the next 30 days, and you will experience a new wave of happiness and fulfillment

230. Your consciousness influences your success – Part I

Consciousness can be referred to as the extent to which you know who you are, your purpose for being alive, and understanding the means or principles by which you will fulfill your purpose.

Simply stated, success is achieving what you set out to accomplish. Your goals are usually twofold. One is the material accomplishment. The other is the "feeling" dimension, which translates as happiness, peace of mind, or some variant of these.

Most persons do not really know who they are. The mystery of life is such that at birth, you had no remembrance of a prior existence. You had no consciousness of what state you were in immediately before birth. Some persons get glimpses of a prior existence. Some believe that the spirit is eternal and never dies.

Some people contend that you come into this world with nothing, and you leave this world with nothing. Thus, perhaps your purpose is to give away your talents and attributes in the service of others. These joyful giving results in your getting whatever you need in this world to experience a good and fruitful life.

When you give materially and spiritually, it is not intended to damage your own prosperity. You have to give to get, but this giving must be done with discernment, and a willing heart, expecting nothing in return.

Perfecting your uniqueness is a powerful concept. You have some special abilities and traits that you excel at more than any other activity. Working your talents with integrity, in the best possible manner, will generate success in your endeavors.

Day 6 review

You have reflected for the past 5 days on different Inspirational Reflections in this book. You should now indicate what insights you got from your reading. List below at least 2 or 3 insights that you got from the Reflections, or information that was reinforced or confirmed.

_____

_____

_____

_____

Day 7 review

You have reflected for the past 6 days on different Inspirational Reflections. To get the best from the material, list below at least 2 areas or particular situations in your life in which you commit to do better.

_____

_____

_____

_____

231. Your consciousness influences your success – Part II

When you achieve a goal, the reward is not merely what you accomplish, but the person you become in the process. Thus, on your journey to be the best that you can be, you reveal your innermost self, and honor your soul. In this thrust, you become an ordinary person who does things extraordinarily.

One of the issues that stifle your consciousness is an excessive identification of your ego. Your ego battles with the five passions of the mind of anger, greed, attachment, vanity, and lust. The deadliest of them is attachment. You find it difficult to detach from your possessions, ideas, money, and loved ones.

Your ego is important as it gives you self-importance, and this is needed to build your self-confidence and self-esteem. However, too much of ego is disastrous. These are five suggestions that can help you from falsely identifying with the negative side of ego:

- Release your need to be right
- Let go of identifying yourself by your achievements
- Let go of your need to win
- Stop being offended
- Let go of your reputation

232. Your consciousness influences your success – Part III

Letting go of your reputation is one of the hardest things to do. When you let go of your reputation, you are not really concerned about what people think of you. You are concerned with being of good character.

Your reputation does not reside within you. It is located in the minds of others. If 25 people speak about you to others, there will be articulated 25 different versions of your reputation. If you are overly concerned with what other people think of you, your actions will be conditioned by their thinking. This is your ego at work. It's an illusion that stands between you and releasing the greatness that is in you.

Do what you do because your inner voice directs you. Stay on purpose, and do not be wedded to the outcome of expectations. Take responsibility for the values that you espouse. That is your character, and it takes precedence over your reputation.

233. Your consciousness influences your success – Part IV

If you have a higher level of consciousness than another person, on the surface, there appears to be no difference between you. Persons with high levels of consciousness do not announce their stage of enlightenment. But when you speak to them, you notice how distinctive they are, compared to people living with ordinary awareness.

People who have a high level of consciousness work with the spirit of intention. They intend that something should occur. There is the intention, and then they put their attention on it. This attention triggers the action necessary to materialize the intention. They do not believe in the traditional meaning of luck. They know that preparation meeting opportunity produce so called "luck."

They design their future life through intention and attention. They take the action, and leave the outcome to the laws of the Universe. They display an attitude of positive expectancy, as there is magic in positive expectancy.

234. Your consciousness influences your success – Part V

Adopt these beliefs, make them operative in your life, and see the magic it produces:

- Believe that there are no limits to what you can dream
- You are unique and spectacular
- Recognize the potential of others, and nurture them
- Understand that all things are possible. Your biggest dreams have not yet been dreamed. Your best ideas are yet to be formulated. Your most successful plans have not yet been drawn.

Consider integrating these values in your life, to generate greater success:

- Reduce your judgment of others
- Focus on what you want, not what you don't want
- Be constantly in a state of gratitude, despite difficulties
- Expect your intentions to be fulfilled
- Establish a daily routine of quieting the mind and going on the inner
- Be generous

- Be inspired to contribute
- Be in connection with your Creator.

235. The magic that is success – Part I

Success occurs when you are living the life you want and love. To manifest your dreams, magic has to occur. In this scenario, magic translates to miracles. Establish your vision, and set out what you want in life. When you do this, miracles will begin to occur, and all your goals will be fulfilled.

When you hear the word "magic" what do you think of? Certainly success does not spring to your mind immediately. Magic triggers images of rabbits being pulled from hats, a woman in a barrel being sawed in two, but emerging alive, and tricks with playing cards. The great magician Harry Houdini explained that magic is achieved through illusion. The illusion is considered to be magic because it appears at first glance to be unexplainable.

The magic of success being discussed here is not an illusion. It is simply magic because it is unexplainable. In fact you can differentiate the magic of success by calling it the miracle of success. Miracles cannot be easily explained. Persons with significant success will admit that their success was aided at times by unexplained circumstances. That is the miracle of success, and it may be useful for you to explore it further.

Day 6 review

You have reflected for the past 5 days on different Inspirational Reflections in this book. You should now indicate what insights you got from your reading. List below at least 2 or 3 insights that you got from the Reflections, or information that was reinforced or confirmed.

_____

_____

_____

_____

Day 7 review

You have reflected for the past 6 days on different Inspirational Reflections. To get the best from the material, list below at least 2 areas or particular situations in your life in which you commit to do better.

_____

_____

_____

_____

236. The magic that is success – Part II

A great deal has been accomplished in my life. However, when the accomplishments are reviewed, it is nothing short of miraculous that things turned out the way they did. Several events have taken place to make it clear that miracles happened very often in my life. The tragedy is that we are not sufficiently alert and sensitive to the interconnecting events that appear to be merely coincidences. Nothing happens by coincidence.

I first became conscious of my miracles through my spiritual transformation at the age of 16. This occurred because of the miracle of substituting Religious Knowledge for General Science at the Cambridge Examination. This training prepared me to accept a heightened spiritual life.

Another miracle was the way in which I was led to do Advanced level Economics that translated to a B.Sc.(Econ) Government Scholarship at Hull University, England. My appointment as Corporate Secretary of the Central Bank evidenced another miracle. Being the first citizen to become the Chief Executive of a commercial bank in Trinidad and Tobago was yet another miracle. There are many other miracles in my life, and particularly in my family relationships.

I am inviting you to look at your countless blessings. Things are sometimes quite rough. So what? Events occur in your life to facilitate your personal growth. Bless the negativity. Also, recognize the miracles. Look back on your life. There are events and occurrences that you cannot explain, but which came at the right moment to help your success. That's the miracle. Acknowledge the miracle, and you open the way for more miracles.

237. The magic that is success – Part III

Miracles don't just happen. They come about because of the other actions you take, and thoughts you generate. When you desire something, get passionate about it and produce massive relevant action to manifest it, then miracles occur. That is, unexplainable events which appear at the right time, seemingly from nowhere, to support your life's design.

There are some principles that you can follow to engender miracles in your life:

- Get to know yourself better
- Be comfortable with whom you are
- Do not be daunted by the false opinions that others have of you
- Always explore different options
- Be flexible but not pliable
- Keep generating decisions
- At every moment, know what is your next step, and take it
- Connect daily with your Creator and cultivate loving relationships

238. The magic that is success – Part IV

You want miracles in your life, but it is just not happening. You have looked at your life, and you are unhappy about certain things. However, you do not seem to be able to take the steps that you know you should take. Why do you not have the courage to act? The answer is simple, yet complex. You are quite comfortable in your present state. You are not hurting sufficiently to get you into new action.

Most times you are not happy with where you are, but it is not hurting intolerably. Other times there is not really hurt. You may desire something different, but you are comfortable with your situation. You are in your comfort zone, and you fear taking a step into the unknown.

You can follow a simple but effective process to encourage the changes and miracles you want:

- Be aware of the change you want
- Strongly commit to the change you want
- Start taking small action steps of change
- Periodically review your progress of change.

239. The magic that is success – Part V

Often you would like something different in your life, but you do not know what it is. The first rule is to discover what it is that is missing, or is present and should not be there. The key is that you have the power to change what is your response to what is happening to you and around you. Change your response and observe the magic of success.

Without your commitment to change little progress can be made. Commitment unleashes forces that propel your initiative, and align other people and situations in your favor. Be resolute and fearless in pursuing the change you want in your life and receive your miracle: that is, your unexpected and unexplained support.

To change you have to do something differently than you have been doing so far. Find that small step of change, and build your future one small step of change at a time. From time to time assess your progress of change and you will know what next needs to be done in your life. Dare to make that change, and receive your miracle of success.

240. Beyond success

The world has changed so much since 1989 that persons have to move from mere effectiveness and success, to greatness. Challenges and complexities confronting today's world is of a significantly different magnitude than in 1989. However, the first stage of effectiveness is still highly applicable in today's world.

To generate success and greatness, you first have to find your own voice, and then inspire others to find their voices. To find your own voice, bring together:

- Your passion
- Your talent
- Your conscience
- Needs of your society

When these elements overlap into a common space, it translates to your unique personal significance, and manifests your own voice.

You must have integrity with yourself. This occurs when you honor your own values. If you believe in something then you must stand up for it. If you don't stand for something, you will fall for anything. Your values can certainly change as you travel life's journey, but at any point in time you must be faithful to the values you then hold. This will help you to become the best that you can be, and catapult you to greatness.

Your uniqueness and strengths grow stronger and stronger in your life. By the same token, weaknesses become amplified, and your closeness to the situation oft times result in blind spots developing. Thus, sometimes you need a personal coach to bring an independent, informed, and experienced viewpoint. This will assist you to optimize your potential, and to let your brilliance shine brightly.

You can continue the life of mediocrity in relation to your potential. Alternatively, you can choose to be a person of destiny, and manifest your greatness. The choice is yours.

Day 6 review

You have reflected for the past 5 days on different Inspirational Reflections in this book. You should now indicate what insights you got from your reading. List below at least 2 or 3 insights that you got from the Reflections, or information that was reinforced or confirmed.

_____

_____

_____

_____

Day 7 review

You have reflected for the past 6 days on different Inspirational Reflections. To get the best from the material, list below at least 2 areas or particular situations in your life in which you commit to do better.

_____

_____

_____

_____

Use the gift of time wisely

241. Success through a sense of self – Part I

You were born innocent which gave you the possibility to do, and be anything you wanted. You were born fearless. You learned to walk, talk, eat and express a creative imagination. Your energy was sometimes so daring that your parents stopped you from doing many things that they rightly thought were dangerous.

The barriers that were erected to stop you from pursuing your curiosity as a child, has stunted your full growth. You were bombarded early in life with many negatives. Research has shown that by age 8 you have been told "no," "don't do this," and "don't do that" on so many occasions, that as an adult you hardly know what you can really do. You have lost your sense of self.

Your negative programming has dulled your sense of adventure, sense of creativity, and the self-confidence and self-esteem to undertake great challenges. You have to find once more the spark of adventure, and courage that you had when you were quite a young child. Re-discover the sense of curiosity you had as a child.

242. Success through a sense of self – Part II

Do you know where you are going with your life? Do you have a sense of purpose? Do you have a sense of self? It is necessary to know who you are, and where you are going to experience a life of joy, happiness and fulfillment.

You have your own unique destiny. You have special talents. Stand up for yourself. Stand up for your neighbor. Stand up for peace, honesty and justice.

Your first responsibility is to yourself. Be in alignment with the Creator, "Be still and know that I am God," as the Psalmist David advised. When you do this, you will begin to realize what your life is all about.

Life is complex. There are no easy and simple answers to satisfy the troublesome questions that arise in your mind. Your finite mind cannot fathom the Infinite Mind and Majesty of God.

The fact of the matter is that you have to live the life you are called to. You can only play the hand that you have been dealt. However, what you possess is your right of choice. You can choose how you respond to your circumstances of life. You can choose to be a victim, or a victor.

You have an obligation to generate your sense of self. This is your birthright. You are designed and engineered with capacity and potential to be your best. When you reclaim your sense of self, you will truly appreciate others, and their needs. Be assured that your relevance depends on the value you can contribute to the needs of others. You are your brother's and sister's keeper. Honor your stewardship.

243. Success through a sense of self – Part III

Consider the following factors that can contribute to your sense of self:

- Revisit the notion of where you came from, and where you are going
- Establish the values that you want to govern your life
- Accept your birthright of potential ability
- Focus on the main accomplishments you desire
- Act with passion, courage and persistence to materialize the dreams of your heart

You can be whatever you want to be. Believe that you have the innate abilities to be what you want to be. Soldier on in the belief of your potential!

244. Success through a sense of self – Part IV

For very many persons there is a conflict in their lives between the pursuit of their spirituality and the requirement to generate sufficient income to meet their needs and that of their family. At a stage in life I had this conflict, but I resolved it after much dialogue, reflection and prayer.

Put simply, I concluded that God is a God of abundance—the earth is His, and the fullness thereof. Consequently, if I am a Child of God, there is no way that God will frown on my own abundance, if I keep a correct relationship with him. Moreover this dichotomy is resolved by Ecclesiastes Ch.10:19, and 1 Timothy Ch. 6:10 that state respectively " …money answers all things," and "For the love of money is the root of all evil."

There is another practical aspect to the discussion. If you feel or find that your wealth is in excess of your needs, give the surplus to the poor, give it to charity, give it to the Church, or give it to some other worthy cause of your choice. Also remember that if you have insufficient money to meet your needs, this can cause you great pain and stress.

245. Success through a sense of self – Part V

Two aspects of success are:

- Do people think that you are a success?
- When do you consider your life to be successful?

What people think of you should not be your primary concern. Your concern is to have integrity. Every person you encounter will have a different version of who you are, and whether you are a success. Ask 30 people what they think of you, and you will get 30 different answers. Thus, to rely on others to validate your success will be confusing and frightening. You have to establish your own understanding of success, and your own sense of self.

Your life is a success from your point of view, when what you want in life has been significantly accomplished. This explains the need for you to establish what will bring happiness to your life.

Day 6 review

You have reflected for the past 5 days on different Inspirational Reflections in this book. You should now indicate what insights you got from your reading. List below at least 2 or 3 insights that you got from the Reflections, or information that was reinforced or confirmed.

_____

_____

_____

_____

Day 7 review

You have reflected for the past 6 days on different Inspirational Reflections. To get the best from the material, list below at least 2 areas or particular situations in your life in which you commit to do better.

_____

_____

_____

_____

246. Success through a sense of self – Part VI

You were born to be happy. One definition of success is that it is an expansion of happiness on your life's journey.

Happiness combines the harmonization of material and spiritual needs. The spirit gives expression in material form. The material form is the manifestation of the spirit's design.

Hence the well known adages, "so within, so without," and "Thy will be done on earth as it is in heaven." You have the challenge to find your voice, to get a sense of self, and live a life of significance.

You can live a life of happiness if your choices are life supporting. Choose wisely and live a life of abundant prosperity, both spiritually and materially.

247. Your reality map limits your success – Part I

You have a map that guides your life. It is internal to your being, and is sometimes called "your internal map of reality." It is called your inner map of reality because you use it as the truth for your living moment by moment

Most of the views expressed in this *Reflective Empowerment,* are not new to you. However, sometimes I present them from a new angle. Anyway, you will only warm to those ideas that fit with your internal map of reality. That map was created from the experiences, joys, hurts, trauma, and exhilaration that you have tasted in your journey from the womb to the present time.

It is natural for the mind to think, analyze, follow logic, and be caught up in dilemma and complexity. However, often you lose sight of the fact that the mind is only a tool, and it is not your essence. The mind structures your internal map of reality to take account of your premier relationship, which is safety in the family.

Your views, values, concerns, hopes, aspirations, vision, and creative spirit are all nurtured, and at the same time destroyed, in the crucible of the family relationship. This is a formation that takes place quite automatically, and often without any formal structure. Thus, you need to become more conscious of your core values, and live in harmony with them.

248. Your reality map limits your success – Part II

In your process of growth, at some particular age, your mind weaves a story about an issue that confronted you then. Say at nine years, something you really wanted and asked for was denied you. Your mind might interpret the situation as rejection. Thereafter, every parallel situation triggers rejection in your mind, and your life and career may be governed by this event. This is unfortunate.

For example, at age 40 you may be still behaving as a nine year old. This is sometimes referred to as the inner child in you. Other examples include public speaking, mathematics, or activities you attempted but at which you were not successful. This interconnection goes deeper, if you were also ridiculed, or teased about your particular inadequacy.

Your new vision is that you must see yourself as, "being the possibility of an adult." An interesting point is that with education, you can see and understand the value of particular concepts and actions, but your internal map of reality prevents you from applying the wisdom to your own life.

These moments of childlike behavior often go unnoticed by you, as over the years you have bought into the childlike behavior. Reflect on whether you are behaving now in some situations as a child, and not as an adult.

249. Your reality map limits your success – Part III

I discovered that in some situations, I was behaving as a child rather than as an adult. I carried my childish consciousness unwittingly into my adult life, due to the original childlike emotions involved. That is one of the reasons for my sharing the information in these Reflections. I have not always been successful in my quest for personal growth. I am still making efforts at transformation, so that I can have the possibility of being adult.

While pursuing a Wisdom Course in 1993 in Atlanta, U.S.A. to understand myself better, I completed an assignment of a pictorial autobiography. The project required that each year of my life be represented pictorially on a page, with a suitable caption.

This was revealing. It showed me how at ages 40, 50 and 60, I was displaying inappropriate behavior of a 9 year, 15 year and 28 year old person. The challenge was for me to shift my internal map of reality, and be an adult.

250. Your reality map limits your success – Part IV

A key insight is that people fail, even when they do things that work for other people. This is so because they don't feel safe changing. This conforms to the model that your internal map of reality defines who you think you are; and how you relate to the rest of the world. This internal reality map generates your entire experience of life, both internally and externally! This map includes your beliefs, values, strategies, ways you filter, store, sort, and retrieve what comes at you from the outside world. You are really a prisoner of the past.

The tragedy is that you only feel safe if your map of reality is intact. While the map worked relatively well in growing up, you are no longer of a younger age, and you have not adjusted to your new environment. You were powerless as a child, or when at a tender age. Today you are an adult as far as your calendar age goes. Work on becoming an adult emotionally to match your chronological age. The objective must be to let your conscious mind override your subconscious child of safety.

What is a practical step that you can take to move forward? A key element is to control your mind, and not let your mind control you. What is involved here is that the mind is so powerful that if you do not keep it in check as a tool, it will become the master.

An analogy will help to clarify this concept. A map is not the territory, it is only a representation of the territory. Thus, your internal map is not the reality, but it represents or depicts the territory. Be mindful that the map is representing the territory accurately.

Day 6 review

You have reflected for the past 5 days on different Inspirational Reflections in this book. You should now indicate what insights you got from your reading. List below at least 2 or 3 insights that you got from the Reflections, or information that was reinforced or confirmed.

_____

_____

_____

_____

Day 7 review

You have reflected for the past 6 days on different Inspirational Reflections. To get the best from the material, list below at least 2 areas or particular situations in your life in which you commit to do better.

_____

_____

_____

_____

Let love flow from your heart

251. Your reality map limits your success – Part V

You alone have the power to interpret your map of reality properly. To do this proper interpretation you have to be the observer, otherwise called the watchman or watcher. As this "witness" becomes more prominent, your mind becomes more of the tool that it is, and you are then able to use the mind adroitly.

Being the observer requires you to find a technique within your value system to quiet your mind. This can be done through contemplative prayer, mediation, quiet time or any similar esoteric practice.

The observer is who you really are. The observer is content and peaceful, and is not wedded to the outcome of your expectations. It just watches whatever happens without emotion or judgment Your tasks it to reclaim your heritage, and merge with the Eternal by practicing more consciously as an "observer."

252. Questions drive your success – Part I

Your life unfolds through the requests you make. If you do not ask for what you want, you will be denied many benefits that are available to you. Review your life and you will notice that you were always making requests, always asking for something you wanted. You asked for food as a young child, you asked to go outside to play. As a teenager, you asked to go out with friends. After leaving school you asked for a job, and then later on you asked to go steady with a loved one.

Asking for what you want is so important, yet most persons were not taught about its rudiments. There are six main elements involved in asking:

- Be clear about what you are asking
- Be circumspect in the way you ask
- Ask of persons who have the power to grant your request
- Be deserving of what you ask
- Have the belief that you will get what you ask for
- Understand that a range of answers is possible

There is the adage that you must be careful for what you ask as you may get it. A friend of mine explained that he kept asking to be a millionaire. He got his wish, but it turned out that he was a millionaire in debt. Clarify exactly what it is you want. You have to be specific to be terrific.

Your parents always told you that it is not only what you ask for, but the way in which you ask for it that is important. You have to ask with humility, while not groveling in the dust. So start asking with more discernment from today.

253. Questions drive your success – Part II

It is not wise to ask for something that you are not entitled to, or for which the person being asked has no authority to grant your request. Moreover, when you deserve what you ask for, you can emit confidence in your asking.

The Holy Scriptures say quite simply: ask and you will receive.

You have to ask in faith believing. If you ask without belief, your request will come over weak. The chances of getting what you want will be reduced. You really cannot get everything that you want, but you can upgrade everything that you have.

Also, in your asking the natural physical laws of the Universe have to be observed. It will be foolhardy to jump from 30 floors high without some form of parachute, and ask that you land safely on the ground. This leads to the other point that faith or belief in what you ask for, without works or the appropriate action, will not be productive. Remember that when you ask for something you have the responsibility to take some related action. There has to be an exchange of energies between the asker and the giver.

254. Questions drive your success – Part III

One of the important points to note is that there are several possible answers to your request. Thus, you must not be wedded to your expectations of the outcome of your asking.

The five possible outcomes when you ask for something are:

- Yes, I will grant your request
- A definite "no"
- Maybe, perhaps, or let me think about it
- A counter proposal: you ask to be given $100 but the counter offer is $80
- An added condition: yes, I agree to your request but you will have to do 'x' for me in return

If asking is so important to your life, why then do you not ask more massively and more aggressively? The simple answer is that you do not appreciate the power of the concept of the question. Suppose you are thinking about asking a question of someone, but you do not actually ask the question. The effect of this is that the answer to your possible question is "no."

Suppose you ask the question, and you get "no" for the answer. You are no worse off than if you did not ask the question. However, it is possible that you might get "yes." The moral of the story is to be brave and ask the question. You have nothing to lose other than your false pride.

255. Questions drive your success – Part IV

There are some other reasons why you do not ask for what you want:

- Lack of knowledge
- Programmed beliefs
- Fear
- Low self-esteem
- Ego

You may not know what to ask for, or you may not know what is available for the asking. Your parents, teachers, and the society have instilled in you that it is not a good thing to ask too many questions.

Based on your past experience, you fear rejection, embarrassment and pain that you get when your request is not entertained. The low-esteem in which you hold yourself, stops you from being proactive in asking questions.

Finally, a big stumbling block is your ego that will be damaged if you do not get what you asked for. You believe that this will make you look foolish, or you will lose the respect of your family, friends and peers. You can override these stumbling blocks. You have the option to ask questions, and there is power in asking questions.

Day 6 review

You have reflected for the past 5 days on different Inspirational Reflections in this book. You should now indicate what insights you got from your reading. List below at least 2 or 3 insights that you got from the Reflections, or information that was reinforced or confirmed.

_____

_____

_____

_____

Day 7 review

You have reflected for the past 6 days on different Inspirational Reflections. To get the best from the material, list below at least 2 areas or particular situations in your life in which you commit to do better.

_____

_____

_____

_____

256. Questions drive your success – Part V

You can take more effective control of your life by asking a series of discerning questions.. Questions can clarify issues, and draw out crucial information. If the question is handled skillfully, it can also be used as a technique to avoid confrontation. You can master the art of asking by using the following elements:

- Know what you want by being clear on your vision, purpose and goals
- Believe that what you are asking for is possible
- Be passionate about what you want—enthusiasm makes all the difference
- When you want to ask and you feel the fear—feel the fear, but ask
- learn from every negative experience, and so become better "askers"
- Be persistent and consistent: if at first your request is not accepted, or acted upon, modify, ask and ask until you succeed.

You can turn your life around by the adroit asking for what you want. Have no regrets for your past actions. Have no fear for your future life. Live in the present moment, and live this day with joy and positive expectancy. What you conceive, truly believe, ask for, and act upon massively, can be achieved.

257. Illusion and success – Part I

There is a view that life is an illusion. This stems from the fact that persons see the same thing quite differently. The argument goes that if the events and items were factual, and real, all persons would see the same thing. While people may see the same thing quite differently, it does not necessarily follow that life is an illusion

Another view is that while life may not be an illusion, it is certainly so for the individual who is not seeing the truth of the matter. Thus, know the truth and be set free from the illusion you have about the matter.

It is the differing interpretations of the truth of the matter that accounts for, among other things, wars, different religions, strained relationships, crime, and cultural biases. Each person has the choice to establish a construct of anything.

If the truth be told, life is so complex that no one person has all the answers; or even understands the magnificence, and glory of the intricate elements of creation. Even medical science has not been able to understand fully the functioning of the human body. Thus, medical science has not been able to provide fully for the body's reaction to disease.

What then is the significance of this concept of illusion of your life? Do you really know what lies behind life? You come into this world in Innocence. You grow up, you achieve, you create great wealth, and then you die leaving everything behind. Are you following an illusion? You will have your own answer: to each his own.

258. Illusion and success – Part II

Are you living an unconscious life? Are you aware of who you are, the way the world (material and spiritual) works, and how you are to operate or exist within it? Many persons are at a stage of indifference, and thereby live a life of unconscious living. Some persons call this misrepresentation, or illusion.

Of course the way you see the world is a function of the way you were programmed to see it. From a baby you were trained to believe certain things. Your parents, teachers, religious leaders, friends, television, cable and other media programmed your beliefs. There is a lot more about the world than you know. Put another way, you have far more potential and internal power than you imagine.

It is a common belief that we are all connected through a spark of Divinity in each of us. Yet you fear that if another wins, you lose. A timeless truth is that when you shift from an obsession to survive, into a compelling commitment to serve, you will experience magnificence in your life. You can generate your unique service by being on purpose, and being true to yourself. Deepen your commitment to be of service, and value to others.

259. The inner game of success – Part I

Do you want to live a life of deep satisfaction and success? Most certainly is probably your answer. However, your life is governed by your unconscious inner programming, and this usually limits and sets boundaries to your success. Be it known, though, that you can make all your dreams come true. You have the potential and spiritual energy to master your life. It's possible. You can do it.

The inner operations of your mind occur at the conscious and subconscious levels. You consciously consider the questions and possibilities of what can happen in your life. You make conscious choices to act and to follow the path of your dreams. The deeper issue is that there is a myriad of programming that operates subtly and unconsciously.

Values about honesty, money, love, eating, anger, depression and other emotions, and core values are set in your internal consciousness: this is done through your family network, friends and teachers.

Many events occurred in your life, and you overlaid them with stories. For example, one of my friends, a medical doctor, signed up for a speech training evaluation. The session ended up with her being trained to sing. She confessed that it was a most liberating experience.

At eight years she went to audition to join her school choir. The Choir Mistress heard a few notes and waved her off as not being suitable to join the choir. This humiliated my friend, and she has lived with the distress all her life. She was clear that she could never sing. This story of an 8 year old had been broken. She can sing. She has reclaimed her voice. You too can overcome bad programming.

260. The inner game of success – Part II

Thoughts are the parents of your words. Words generate actions. Actions develop habits. Habits create a lifestyle. To change your life style you have to change your habits. The change must go all the way back to the thinking, the inner response. You need to align your inner game with your vision of success in order to deliver the life you want.

Your thinking is conditioned by how you have been programmed from birth. The way you think and the communication that results, play an important part in your life. You think continuously. You may not understand the process of your mind and senses, but you have the evidence of their existence.

When you know the truth about the power of your thinking you will get the insight that you create your universe with your thinking. Your power is so great that there is nothing you cannot do, if you earnestly put your mind and resources to it. Thus, your mind set is the key to the success results you get in life.

If you believe that life is something that happens and you cannot change it, this leaves you powerless. Rather believe that your world, and everything in it is created, either through your actions or inactions. This in turn is powered by your inner game of thinking. This view will give you access to change what you do not like about your life. You can birth THE CHAMPION that is within you.

Day 6 review

You have reflected for the past 5 days on different Inspirational Reflections in this book. You should now indicate what insights you got from your reading. List below at least 2 or 3 insights that you got from the Reflections, or information that was reinforced or confirmed.

_____

_____

_____

Day 7 review

You have reflected for the past 6 days on different Inspirational Reflections. To get the best from the material, list below at least 2 areas or particular situations in your life in which you commit to do better.

_____

_____

_____

_____

OVERALL CONCLUSION

Empowerment is the strength within you to be and do what you visualize. Empowerment is triggered when you have the freedom to do what makes you happy and the power to get it done. With modern technology you are no longer isolated with limitations. You can now be connected to all human knowledge, and empowered by infinite possibilities. You empower yourself when you choose to design and control your life, rather than let apathy and complacency rule.

You have completed the readings for 365 days. If you followed the program faithfully, you should now be much more effective than 12 months ago. Also, You should have a better grasp on designing, and living the life you truly want. You have been empowered to live your passion powerfully.

You are amazing and unique. Let your brilliance shine through, and always persist to accomplish what you desire. You have the POWER. Use your empowerment wisely.

Printed in the United States
By Bookmasters